the Relationship Guide to make Him or Her commit

The Master Love Collection: A True Poetic Love Experience

Julius F. Rafael

authorHOUSE®

AuthorHouse™ LLC
1663 Liberty Drive
Bloomington, IN 47403
www.authorhouse.com
Phone: 1-800-839-8640

Published by AuthorHouse   08/28/2013

ISBN: 978-1-4817-7625-7 (sc)
ISBN: 978-1-4817-7624-0 (hc)
ISBN: 978-1-4817-7623-3 (e)

Library of Congress Control Number: 2013912564

CONTENTS

Prologue ix

Section I:
The Soul Mate—The approach, making him or her commit

CHAPTER 1—WHEN WE MEET / THE APPROACH (Approaching her) 3
- *Speed Dating* 5
- *Dealing with Rejection* 7
- *Time to Call a Woman* 7
- *The Short Memory* 8

CHAPTER 2—VIRTUOUS WOMAN (Making her commit) 11
- *Maximize her Potential* 12
- *Help her Reach her Goals* 13
- *Learn Her Style* 14
- *The Gold Digger* 14
- *The Cute Chic* 15
- *Ms. Plus Size* 15
- *The Fun Girl* 16
- *Ms. Career Oriented* 17
- *The Spiritual Woman* 18

CHAPTER 3—REAL MAN (Making her commit) 20
- *Swagger /Distinguished Gentleman* 21
- *Supporter* 24
- *Provider/ Head of Household* 24
- *Pride/ Stand up to a Challenge* 26
- *Think like a Man, and Not like a Boy* 26

Chapter 4—My Wants and My Needs (Making him commit).......... 28
- *Equally Yoked*.. 29
- *Getting out of his "Friend Zone"*................................... 32
- *Promiscuous*.. 34
- *Her Wants and her Desires*.. 35
- *Overly Anxious & Jealous*... 36
- *Woman's Weight*... 37
- *Emotional Intelligence*.. 39
- *Your Kids*.. 40
- *His Issues*... 40
- *Why men take on the "Baby Daddy Role"*...................... 41
- *The Pregnancy Trap: "The Ole Keep a Brother Baby"*
  baby daddy role continued 42

Section II:
The Chasing Game—The cheating man, temptation, avoiding her Friend Zone

Chapter 5—Why do I Cheat?/ Why do Men Cheat? 47
- *The Conquest* 49
- *The Roster* 50
- *His Peers* 51
- *Self-Esteem* 52
- *The Flesh*... 53
- *She needs some "Get Right"* 54

Chapter 6—The 80/20 Rule (Battling Temptation) 57
- *His Temptation*.. 59
- *Macho Man Factor / the Victimized Man*........................ 59
- *Her Temptation* 60
- *The Female Attraction*... 61

Chapter 7—The Friend Zone (Avoiding her "Friend Zone") 62
- *Getting Out of her "Friend Zone"* 64
- *Reverse & Benefit from the "Friend Zone"* 65

Section III:
The Intimacy Chapters—How to make her sexually commit
The TOP TEN positions that guarantee's her orgasm

CHAPTER 8—LOVING YOU / ASKING WHY 71
  • *One Night Stand and the "Pad Swagger"* 73

CHAPTER 9—BEING INTIMATE 75
  • *Becoming the Big "D" Bandit* 78
  • *Getting her "D" whipped* 79

CHAPTER 10—THE ART OF PASSION 80
  • *Sex the Art of Love Making* 81
  • *The Top Ten Sex Positions (Make her Commit)* 81

Section IV:
Love and Marriage—Making her a Keepsake

CHAPTER 11—TIME 89
CHAPTER 12—THE HOLIDAYS 93
CHAPTER 13—YOUR ROMANCE 95
CHAPTER 14—CORPORATE MERGER 98

Section V:
The Answer—Trust, Listen, Understand, Believe

CHAPTER 15—THE ANSWER 107
  • *Understand and Overcome Stubbornness* 109
  • *Trust and Overcome Temptation* 110
  • *Listen and Believe* 111

Section VI:
Learn his sport in Plain English
The Woman's Sports Cheat Sheet (Football, Basketball, Baseball)

Men and their Sports (What's the Big Deal?).................................... 117

Football Cheat Sheet for Women.. 119
- *What does 1st, 2nd, 3rd and 4th down mean?*......................... 120
- *Football Offence in Plain English (11 men on the field)* 124
- *Football Defense in Plain English (11 men on the field)* 125
- *Keeping the Score* 126

Basketball Cheat Sheet for Women... 129
- *The Starting Lineup: (from Tall to Short)* 130
- *Things to know in Basketball*... 131

Baseball Cheat Sheet for Women.. 134
- *Baseball Offence in plain English*...................................... 135
- *Baseball Defense in plain English*...................................... 136
- *Things to know in Baseball*.. 136

Acknowledgements.. 141

PROLOGUE

While obtaining my Master's Degree in Business, I have discovered that businesses and relationships are very similar. To maintain a business and to sustain a successful relationship, it takes hard work. After being with a woman for more than a decade and never fully committing to her, I finally figured out why I did not want to commit. In this book, I mention reasons why I and other men such as myself don't commit. This book also list several strategies that a woman can use if she wants a man to commit to her. I have dated 100's of women, and while dating these women, I have discovered what they want. These women have been either, married or single. In this book, I have also listed several ways to sexually satisfy women with my Top Ten Sex Positions.

The "Master Love Collection: the Relationship Guide to make him or her commit," is a collection of poems followed by a complete explanation that truly explains how to get men and women to commit to each other. Each poem is a unique piece of work that has been recited throughout the United States. This book covers but not limited to: the cheating man, how to approach a woman, and how to sexually satisfy her. This book is not intended to be read in chronological order because it touches on several different relational topics. For example, the reader can skip to the end of this book and visit the Woman's Sport Cheat Sheet.

The Woman's Sport Cheat Sheet explains why men love sports, and how a woman can get closer to their man by learning his sport. In this section, the "The Woman's Sports Cheat Sheet," explains a man's sport in plain English. With this Sports Cheat Sheet, women will better understand their man by learning the sport he loves, and this will give her commitment points. As a poet, author and a business man, several women have fallen in love with my poetic pieces, and by writing this book, I can share these same poetic pieces with the world. Upon purchasing this book, you can recite or give these poetic pieces to your significant other to gain commitment points.

This book is centered on love and it also has a spiritual feel, and women are uplifted: emotionally, physically and mentally. The "Master Love Collection: the Relationship Guide to make him or her commit," helps women understand the thought process of a man because in certain sections of this book, I speak directly to men. This book is unlike any other book because it speaks directly to men and women, and couples can read this book together. This book also explains the institution of marriage and how to keep a healthy marriage. It also has biblical references that explain how God intended men and women to live coherently together. To get a full concept of this book, it's important to visit each poetic piece first, and then visit the poetic explanation which explains the poetic piece.

SECTION I

The Soul Mate*—The approach, making him or her commit*

CHAPTER 1—WHEN WE MEET / THE APPROACH

(the Man's guide how to approach her)

Yearning to meet you, I have always searched to find someone like you;
Seeing such beauty for the very first time, on a scale from one to ten, you are more
than a dime;
Approaching you like the angel that you are, thinking, have we met before?
It seems, maybe in a dream?

When we first met,
I instantly noticed your Independent sexiness, for you, it seems to come so
effortless;
Approaching you, thinking, how do I past this test?

You have an elegant sex appeal; your attraction is such a thrill;
Thinking of the right thought, because Independence is what you are all about;
Stepping to you with such Confidence & Pride,
This is what is inside of me & it will not hide;

EXCUSE ME Ms, EXCUSE ME Ms!!!

My heart tells me that you are an inspiration, something like a queen who rules a
strong **nation**;
I am not trying to bore you with useless **conversation**,
But you are a wonderful, Godly **creation**;
Trying not to approach you, but I can't fight this burning **sensation**;
Nubian Queen, I have to ask, can I have your contact **information**?
So anxiously to speak, I almost became weak,
But you may be my wife, that's why I took this leap.

When we Meet

THE EXPLANATION = THE INTERPRETATION: WHEN WE MEET

This poetic piece discusses the art of meeting and approaching a woman. While obtaining a Master's Degree in business, I have learned, men can use the same strategies and techniques a business use to attract customers, to attract women. Men, the first thing to remember when it comes to women is: as a man, you have to be in DEMAND. For example, when a business starts, to be successful, it must find a product to sell that is in demand. Once there is a strong demand for the company's products, the company would have several customers. Men, if we appear to be in demand, the more customers/women we will have. The way we approach a woman is essential to obtaining the goal of making her commit to us. We should simply start with a respectful light conversation by giving her a compliment. After the compliment we can let her know that we are interested in getting to know her. If she declines our offer, we should simply move on. When we approach a woman, it is our sales pitch. For example, if we see a salesman trying to sale a product, and that salesman has dirty clothes, and dusty shoes, we would not be quick to buy from that salesman. Another way to look at dating and the ways you should approach a woman is: examine how a successful business operates. If you are a business owner, and your company is fairly new, as a business owner, you would need some type of investment to keep your company running. To attract customers, a new company must spend money on advertisement, equipment or merchandise, and the business must have a place to operate.

A company must also spend money to create its brand name and image. When it comes to meeting women, you need to have an attractive brand or image. To build your brand, you must advertise; you would have to spend a little money on equipment, whether it's nice clothes, or a nice car or a nice home. You would also need a place to operate. After a couple of conversations with a woman, you should ask her for a date, and while you are out on a date, this is your time to fully operate and close the sale with this woman. Like a business, if you want a woman to be a customer of your love, you must appear to have some type of upkeep and success about yourself. This would be further explained in the "Real Man" chapter. If you leave your house and go where a woman may be present, you should try your best to look decent and attractive. When women first meet a man, the first thing a woman notice is a man's shoes as well as his overall appearance. Upon meeting a woman, in seconds, she knows if she wants to sleep with you or not. If she wants you to approach her, she will make eye contact, and once she makes eye contact, it's more than likely that she wants you to ask her for her phone number.

Speed Dating

As men, we should approach women as if we were "Speed Dating." Speed Dating is when two individuals meet each other and talk for 60 seconds or less. Upon meeting women, we need to remember not to say anything that may offend them, but within 60 seconds or less, we should try to make them feel good about themselves. We should try to make ourselves seem very attractive by telling them what they want to hear. We can start a conversation by asking a woman an open ended question such as: do I know you, or did I go to school with you? Another open ended question could be: are you some kin to someone you may know? These are open ended questions that are simply "pick up lines," and they are great conversation starters. All women are different, so men, in 60 seconds, we should always try to learn as much as possible about that woman. After an initial conversation, we can introduce some things about ourselves that they may find interesting.

As mentioned earlier, we should always approach a woman as if we were speed dating. If we are in the club, or in another social gathering, we should talk to as many women as possible, but we should make sure that we are respectful when we branch off to different women. Although we may approach many women, we need to make all of them feel important. So, it may be necessary to be very discrete when approaching different females. As men, dating is part of finding our soul mate. If a woman gets upset because you talk to other women, explain to her that you are speed dating and you are in search of your ideal mate. Let her know that it's never personal when it comes to dating multiple women because you are not in a relationship.

If a woman works at your place of employment, or if she is seen on a routine basis, it is best that you approach her at the right time. It is not always recommended to date a woman at your place of employment because once you get to know her, and you no longer want to pursue her, she may create problems for you while at work. Men, if you want to date a woman that you routinely see, you should not approach her until after a couple of encounters. Due to the fact that you may see her on a routine basis, you should be patient, and after two weeks or so, you should consider asking her for her number. Sometimes, it's not ideal to get involved with co-worker, but if you are seriously interested in her, the first thing that you should do while pursuing her is to NOT make it known that you are overly interested in her. You should simply have a couple of casual conversations with her, then when the time is right, you should ask her for her number; it is very important that you do not ask her for her number after the first conversation because she is frequently seen. There would be other opportunities to get her number.

When a man takes this approach with the routinely seen woman, that woman will question: why didn't I fully catch his attention? Not fully catching your attention will show her that you are very important and you are in high demand. While dating, you should never be readily available to a woman. Never being readily available reassures that you are in DEMAND. When a man is busy, a woman will start to question why doesn't he have time to fully chat with me? Although you are fully interested in her, it's important to let her question if you are fully interested. She will desire you more because she will see you as a challenge, and she will desperately want you. When you finally show interest, she will fall right into your hands. Women are desirable creatures who love attention, and when a woman is finally recognized, she will feel desirable, especially when her man at home does not give her the types of compliments and attention she thinks she deserves.

Dealing with Rejection

If a woman declines to provide her contact information, or if she declines to accept your contact information, you should keep your head up and move on to the next woman. As men, we should respect her wishes by leaving her alone after she declines our offer. We can thank her for her time, and wish her a nice day. If we are polite to her, and respect her whishes, she may wonder what type of man she has just turned down. She may wonder, what type of man you are, although she is involved in a relationship. Some women may be very disrespectful, but if we let her know that she doesn't have to be disrespectful, she should understand. Men, we should never baffle with a woman after she turns us down; we should simple move on to the next. Upon rejection, we should always keep our head up, and walk away with pride.

If a woman is in a relationship, we can still offer our number for networking purposes. We can make a suggestion to her and let her know that, if her relationship situation changes, she can give us a call. If she declines the friendship suggestion, simply cut the conversation very short. Thank her for her time, and move on. Upon rejection, it's important to realize that you may not be what she wants, and you should treat the rejection as if it was a favor from her. You don't want her to lead you on, waste your time or your money. Simply, move on to the next woman. We need to take the approach that maybe this woman might have mental problems; she may have 5 or 6 kids fathered by 3 different men or she may have an estrange ex-boyfriend that would create unwanted problems. We do not need this baggage in our lives. As men, we should understand: we do not think that every woman is attractive, so every woman may not find us attractive. We should never be intimidated to approach any woman because we are designed to be leaders, and no matter how attractive a woman thinks she is, there is a man for her, and you might be that man.

Time to Call a Woman

When you first meet a woman, she knows if she wants to sleep with you or not. Men, we can have several one-night stands because women love sex as much as we do. It all starts with your initial approach. You have to have self-confidence, and when you show a sign of weakness, you are considered to be weak or lame. The time limit to call a woman all depends. If you call a woman within two hours, it shows that you may be very interested in her, but this may backfire because you don't always know if she really likes you are not. If you wait a day or two before calling her, she will know that you have a life, and you took time out of your busy schedule to contact her.

If you take too long to call her and if she really likes you, she will make it aware that you took a long time to call. If you call her right away, it is important that you make sure that you do not continue to call her all the time. When men constantly reach out to women they first meet, she might feel as if that man doesn't have a life, and he is overly anxious to get to know her. You should make sure that you don't fall in the category as being a "**Bug-a-Boo.**" Women hate men who take the Bug-a-Boo role. The Bug-a-Boo role is a role that men take when they are very anxious to spend time with that woman or get to know her. A Bug-a-Boo will call this woman at least five times a day, and at least 10 times a week. Being a Bug-a-Boo leaves a woman to think that you are controlling or you don't have a life.

As mentioned above, it doesn't actually matters when to call a woman, but it all depends on the initial conversation. Women love for their minds to be stimulated, and they like an intriguing man. It's best to try to get to know a woman by asking her where she's from, or does she have any kids, etc. The biggest mistake men make when they first talk on the phone with a woman is to talk about sleeping with her. If you have a respectable, interesting conversation with her, and if you get to know her, she will be more than willing get to know you and eventually have sex with you.

The Short Memory

Men, we need to have a very short memory. After we call a woman, and she does not show any interest, we need to move on. If we move on, it will make that woman desire you more. After receiving a woman's number, and once a call is made, it is recommended that you use the "**Three Attempt Rule**." The Three Attempt Rule is when a man attempts to reach out to that woman three times, and after the last attempt, and the woman does not respond, move on to the next woman. Never waste your time and energy on a woman who doesn't want you!! Although a woman may not initially show interest, it may be a good idea to hold on to her number for a month or two, depending on the situation. Upon receiving her number, you should hold on to it because at that given time, she may be tied up with other things in her life. You may want to keep her number as a keepsake. When you keep her number and call her in the future, you may catch her in a vulnerable state. When we catch her in a vulnerable state, whether she is fresh out of a relationship or if she just wants to have a companion, you may have the opportunity to sleep with her. Although a pursuit is important, if she doesn't want you, she just doesn't want you. If your pursuit last for a long time, it decreases your chances of ever getting to know her. Time is very important, and if you do not value your own time, how can she value it?

Men, when approaching a woman, we should always remember to have self-confidence. We should become the chase, not the chaser. When we become the chase, woman will sleep with you more quickly. When you are considered the chase, women will pay your bills, they will do anything for you, and it doesn't matter how attractive that woman thinks she is; when she chases a man, she wants that man. She will do almost anything to be with him. In the "Real Man" chapter it's a complete explanation of how you can make a woman chase you. As men, we should understand that there are several different women in this world and we have options.

We should always remember one thing: what one woman will not do, there is always a woman who will. As a man, you should constantly work on self improvement, and once this happens, you will instantly become very desirable. When a man is established, he has a lot of options. This is why women desire married men. Married men appear to be very successful and established. To become desirable, it's important to chase success and not women!!!! This simple concept should be deeply rooted in a man's mind, and when time permits, he should show a woman a since of interest. If you have your overall appearance together, and you appear to have it going on, you will easily attract women. It's important to keep a positive attitude while approaching a woman. A very attractive woman usually does not leave her home without having herself together, and as a man, *you should never leave your home without having a since of confidence.* On a daily basis, you may encounter women. You can meet a woman anywhere; you can approach them at grocery stores, at gas stations, at the gym, at sporting events, at nightclubs, at open bars, at local parks or at church.

CHAPTER 2—VIRTUOUS WOMAN

(the Man's guide to make her commit)

Loose and never up tight, my Virtuous Woman. Your mind and body is so educated, with your soul so sophisticated. You are a Nurturer, a Mother as well as a Sensational Lover. While acting as one, you are a Lawyer, a school Teacher, a lovely Doctor, a business Woman, or a professional Caregiver, and you find time to be a *Wife*. With a superb business Look, when it comes to being Strong, you write the Book. Virtuous woman you are, Love, you shine like a midnight Star. Better known as Complexity, full of Sexuality, you are tamed with such Curiosity. A Woman, smart and full of talent; Nubian in nature, you are a goddess turned into an earthly Queen with beauty that sings. A first lady of a Great Nation, Virtuous Woman you are a wonderful creation. A gift sent from the heavens. A gift that keeps on giving, only you understanding what it means to give birth, the creator named you Mother, as you dwell this Earth.

-My Virtuous Woman

THE EXPLANATION = THE INTERPRETATION: VIRTUOUS WOMAN

The Virtuous Woman poetic piece was written to inspire and uplift women. Once a woman shows interest and if she decides that she wants to date you, it's time for you to help her reach her "Virtuous Woman" status. Men, upon meeting a woman, you should ask her questions about herself; you should start by asking open ended questions. You should ask her what does she likes to do or what are her career goals. Once you know her goals, you can help her to reach her goals. Women want to feel sexy and every woman is Virtuous in their own unique way. It's best to let her know that she is not only sexy, but she is also intelligent. Even though she may not be your ideal mate in the beginning, you should encourage her to make minor changes to herself, but you should never over commit your desires. For example, if a man continues to press a woman to change, she may be resentful towards him. When the resentment starts, she may place extra demands on the relationship. She would always need instant gratification, making it difficult to please her.

Maximize her Potential

A man should let a woman find herself, and he should continue to motivate her. When it comes to motivating her, it's important to learn what makes her feel Virtuous. Men, we should help women reach their maximum potential, and we should let them pick their career path. When it comes to women, we should never put added pressures on them to make them be something that they are not. For example, a woman who wants to be a School Teacher does not want to be a Medical Doctor, and we shouldn't force this on her. We should encourage our women to pursue their dreams by helping them maximize their potential. If a woman wants to be promiscuous, let her be promiscuous. She may feel as if this is her niche, and the more she is desired by other men, the more Virtuous she may feel. This is usually seen in Gold Digging woman. These women are promiscuous because men will pay their bills for sexual favors. With the Gold Digger, the more men she has, the more Virtuous Woman she perceives to be. Women make a major mistake when they are promiscuous and think that they can act like a man. They make a mistake because men can sleep around, but women are emotional creatures and they tend to get their emotions evolve when they sleep around. Men, we should remember, when dealing with a promiscuous woman, you can't turn a "Promiscuous Woman into a House Wife." Although women and men each have a past, if a woman wants to continue to be promiscuous, let her be promiscuous. If she wants to change, motivate her to become independent. We should tap into a woman's mind and help her uplift herself by bringing out her true Woman Hood.

Help her Reach her Goals

It's important to learn what your woman want, and encourage her to pursue her goals. Every woman has a goal in life and when we find out her goals, we should reward her for attempting to achieve her goals. Reaching her goals will make her feel "Virtuous." Some women seek a good man who will take care of them and make them feel like a princess or a queen, and once they find this man, they feel like they are the Virtuous Woman. Women are very unique and curious. They are also complex and emotional. They are nurtures by design, and they want a man who will help them to be complete.

We should encourage a woman to beautify herself by getting her hair and nails done. We should also help her stay trendy by motivating her to purchase the latest fashions. If possible, you can take her shopping; treat her and buy her clothes or shower her with gifts that make her feel special. In this poetic piece, it says: "you are a gift that keeps on giving," this means that the woman can provide the man with unprecedented gifts such as kids, advice or support. It's vital that you let a woman know that she is a gift and she is virtuous in her own way. Although it's not always necessary to treat a woman by taking her shopping or purchase her gifts, you can be charming and let her know how wonderful and intelligent she is. Once this happens, she will want to continue to receive these charming gestures from you. She will try her best to beautify herself because she would enjoy the compliments she receives. Men, we should charm and continue to feed women with gifts, romantic moments, and interesting conversations about their goals. We should let them know that they are Virtuous in their own unique way.

Learn Her Style

Make your woman feel as if she is your "Virtuous Woman." When you make a woman feel as if she is your Virtuous Woman, she will love to be around you. We need to study our women, and learn what makes her feel beautiful and intriguing. Like men, there are no two women that are the same, so getting to know her is vital when trying to make her commit. As mentioned earlier, there is the Gold-Digger. Then, there is the Cute Chic, Ms. Plus Size, the Fun Girl, Ms. Career Oriented and the Spiritual Woman. There may also be a woman who has a mixture of all these characteristics. All of these women with these characteristics want to feel as if they are the Virtuous Woman. As mentioned earlier, even if a man thinks that his woman is not completely there yet, and she has not reached her Virtuous Woman status, you should continue to flatter her with compliments, and let her talk about herself.

The Gold Digger

We should study our woman. For example, if a woman desires a man with a lot of money, we can perceive to have a lot of money until we sleep with her, and after we sleep with her, we can leave her alone, especially if we don't have the financial resources that we perceive to have. Spending money on the Gold Digger woman makes her feel as if she is in control, but a Gold Digger is a Gold Digger. She is only out to spend your money, and after she exhausts all of your funds, she will leave you. With this woman, she feels Virtuous because of the men she dates. When there is another man in her life, she will pursue the man who has the most money because she is in pursuit of being Virtuous. It's best to spend just enough money to make her feel as if she is in control, but after you get what we are looking for, whether it's sex or something else, you should leave her alone. If you tend to stick around the Gold Digging woman, it's a major mistake because once she finds a man with more money, she will leave you.

The Cute Chic

If we date a very attractive woman, we have to let her know that she is beautiful as well as intelligent. When dating the Cute Chic, we must point these things out because she wants to be appreciated for more than her good looks. Like all women, the Cute Chic wants to feel like she is a Virtuous Woman. With the very attractive Cute Chic, it is important that some of her flaws are also mentioned. Let her know that as a man, you are not overly consumed by her good looks, and she is just another woman. Make her chase you, and let it be known that she needs you more than you need her. The Cute Chic attracts several men, and if you let her know that she has work to do to stay cute, she will desire you more. She desires this type of man because he will be a challenge for her; she will try to prove that she is a Virtuous Woman, and she will easily commit to you.

Ms. Plus Size

Women come in all shapes and sizes, and big girls need love too!!! With Ms. Plus size, you should always tell her that she is sexy and intelligent. If she is insecure about her weight, you should try to motivate her to eat right and stay in the gym, but if you desire a small girl when you have Ms. Plus Size, you should leave this big girl alone. If a big girl is happy with being big, or if she finds it very difficult to lose weight, you should never put extra emphasis and pressure this woman to lose weight. As a man, you should motivate her, but never over coach her to be something that she is not. NOTE: If a woman is too big, and if you are not attracted to big girls, the best thing to do is leave her alone because someone who loves big women may enter her life and treat her they way she supposed to be treated.

You should uplift Ms. Plus Size and let her know that although she is a plus size woman, she is still beautiful. When this happens, this would motivate her to strive to lose her weight or she may just want to continue to stay big and sexy. With the plus size woman, you should never tell her that she is too fat, but you can have an honest opinion about her size. You should tell her that she is thick, but she will be even sexier if she looses a couple of pounds. As men, we can tell Ms. Plus Size that we like a woman with a little meat on their bones, but she would be even sexier if she loses a little weight. We can even try working out with her to motivate her to lose weight. Big girls usually know how to treat a man better than skinny girls, anyway. The plus size woman will cook for a man, and they usually are not very high maintenance. They usually have their own money, and they don't require a man to spend a lot of money on them, and the best part of all, they usually have the best oral sex. When a man make a big girl feel as if she is the Virtuous Woman, she will completely take care of him, and she will always stay committed to him.

The Fun Girl

With the Fun Girl, it's important to understand that she just wants to have fun!! As men, we should give her what she wants, and that's just a fun time. These women can be found anywhere, but they are usually found in the club or your local bar. The Fun Girl is never looking for a commitment, but like all women, she desires to be the Virtuous Woman. To make her feel like the Virtuous Woman, you should feed all of her fantasies. If she likes to drink, you should purchase drinks for her. If this woman likes to go out to the club, sometimes it won't hurt to give her money to go out. If this woman likes to smoke marijuana, it's good to let her smoke marijuana, and it may be necessary to purchase the drug for her. The worst thing a man can do when dating the Fun Girl is to try to make her change and commit. When this happens, the Fun Girl may feel as if you are trying to be her father. Although sometimes it's necessary to try to get her to get serious about her life, she doesn't want to feel like she is dating her father. She is only looking to have a good time. She wants to have a lot of sex, drink and smoke, and most of the time, at your expense. As men, we should try to motivate her to get her life together, but we should never force her to do so. We should have fun and enjoy the ride with this party girl, and we should always remember that she may be here today and gone tomorrow. She might want to have fun with another man and leave you alone. When she leaves you alone, you should always remember to stay alert and expect her to call or text you one day. After not hearing from this woman for awhile, and once she reaches out to you, you should plan a date with her.

Let her know that she was missed, but you should not sound anxious to spend time with her. Once this happens, she will know that you have been preoccupied with your time, and she would be excited to go on a date with you. The Fun Girl will appreciate you by making her feel Virtuous. With the Fun Girl, it is truly a cat and mouse game. You should suddenly stop hanging out with her, and you should stop taking her calls. When this happens, she will start to miss you. She would eventually want to commit to you because of the fun times, especially when you dominate her in the bedroom.

Ms. Career Oriented

The career oriented woman may have certain values that she looks for in a man. To get a career oriented woman to commit, you must learn her wants and needs. You must also tell her what she wants to hear. Most career oriented women are women who are very independent and strong. They do not look for a man to take care of them, and they have a true since of Woman Hood. These women are attracted to two types of men. She will be attracted to a man that mirrors her success and a man who is the complete opposite of her. Men, this is why you would usually see a career oriented women with a man who has thuggish characteristics. When the career oriented woman dates a man who is the complete opposite of her, he usually dominates in the bedroom. The bedroom is the time she can be stripped of her perceived dominance and she can show her submissive side.

When dating Ms. Career Oriented, it may be necessary to bend the truth by telling her how successful you are. This is fine in the beginning stages of the relationship because after she experience a good time with you, she will overlook the fact that you do not have it going on the way you said you did. With Ms. Career Oriented, it's important to make her fall in love with your sex, charm and your charisma. When this happens, she will fall right into your arms. With the career oriented woman, you should never be readily available for her, but when time is permitted, it's important to show her a good time. Fellas, if we don't have a good job, we should let this woman know that we are completely independent, and we can stand on our own two feet. We should never show that we are venerable when it comes to our financial situation. With independent strong women, it's important to keep our self-confidence because this woman may be very intimidating. Being intimidating usually leaves this woman single, but when dating this type of woman, you should remember these three rules. 1.) You should attempt to dominate her pussy by sexing her like she has never been sexed before. 2.) You should establish a relationship that speaks independence. 3.) Always keep a positive outlook on life and capitalize on swagger and confidence.

The Spiritual Woman

Spiritual women usually have positive values, and they usually have the ideal characteristics of the Virtuous Woman. These women may have decent careers; they may be good mothers, and they may know how to cook. When dating the Spiritual Woman, it's best to become friends with her, and while being her friend, you should make her feel like a Virtuous Woman. When talking to her, you shouldn't initially ask her for a date. You should be patient and find out her interests. If she is your church member, you would most likely see her on a regular basis. After a good friendship is established with the Spiritual Woman, you should then ask her out on a couple of dates. Even spiritual church women want to be romanced, but most of them may want to wait until they are married to have sex. The Spiritual Woman loves a man who is active in church or if he is very close to his maker, God. Men, it's always good to be friends with the Spiritual Woman, but you should make sure that you do not fall in the Friend Zone. With the Spiritual Women, you have to be very patient. When dating this type of woman, you should work on your spirituality, whether it's joining church ministries or learning God's word. Men, it's important for you to stay mindful, although there are some decent women in church, all so called spiritual church women are not always good. Some church woman may go to church, but like any other woman, they may not have positive values of your ideal Virtuous Woman.

We can find a Virtuous Woman anywhere. Women love to be thought of as a complete woman, but you should have a complete balance when it comes to treating a woman like she is your Virtuous Woman. If you are overly nice while in pursuit of a woman, you will set yourself up for failure because women love a challenge. There are different types of women, and you should always have a since of pride while dating. Although a woman is perceived to be "Virtuous," you should make her prove that she is your Virtuous Woman. Proving to be the Virtuous Woman does not mean that this woman constantly competes for your love, but she should be required to do things to win you over. When this happens, she will always remember that she has worked hard for your love, and she would think twice about losing you. Once a man has established this relationship, it will be difficult for another man to steal your woman's heart. Men, if you apply these techniques that are mentioned in this chapter, you wouldn't have a problem making any type of woman commit.

Chapter 3—Real Man

(Man's guide to make her commit)

A Man that is not full of too much pride,
you have that deep understanding of what it means to provide,
that's why you have me by your side.

The things you whisper in my ear are so sweet;
your smooth swagger swept me off my feet.

A distinguished Gentleman, a Real Man;
no other woman can love you better than I can.

A father and head of this household,
with your touch making me unfold.

Thanking God for sending me a gracious King,
things you do makes my soul Sing.

You are my Adam and I am your Eve,
you are my support system that helps me to Believe.

I am not trying to seduce you; I am just explaining that I Love You.

So strong, when it comes to a challenge, you always take a stand.
When it comes to loving me, you understand, that's why you are a . . . .

-Real Man

THE EXPLANATION = THE INTERPRETATION: REAL MAN

This poetic piece was written in a woman's voice, and it explains everything a woman desires in a man. Most women want a man who has the characteristics that are listed in this poem. If a man posses these characteristics, he will easily make a woman commit. Women are very different from men, and they love a man who helps them to be complete. They seek a man for comfort and companionship. They also want a man who carries his own weight. To get a woman to fully commit, you must have swag. Your swag is very important because it capitalizes on your uniqueness. When men tap into their swag, a woman will stay focused on him. If a woman loves a man's swag, she will instantly fall in love.

Swagger /Distinguished Gentleman

Men, in this poetic piece, it states, "your smooth swagger swept me off of my feet," it's important to focus on establishing your identity by tapping into your unique swag. God made all of us with a special uniqueness about ourselves, and we should be confident in who we are. Whether you are married or single, the ideal swag can make or break a relationship. Once a woman is intrigued by a man's swag, she will find herself opening up to him. Because of his swag and uniqueness, she would be in a complete trance. When it comes to meeting and dealing with women, your confidence is also the virtue of your success, and it's important to have confidence in your swag. For several years, I have noticed some of the most unattractive men who get the most beautiful women based off their confidence and their swag. If you learn the true meaning of swagger, you would be very surprised how easily it is to sleep with women. When a woman loves a man's swag they would do anything to please him. They would commit all types of sexual acts, buy him gifts and they would want to marry him.

My father, my uncles and other male family members were all known womanizers before they found their ideal soul mate. These men womanized women for years! My father showed me how to womanize a woman; several women wanted to marry him. He would have these women buy him gifts, take him out on dates, and provide a place for him to live. But when he found his ideal soul mate, he decided to focus on one woman and settled down. When asked about his womanizer techniques, he agreed that all women flock to him because of his swag.

When you find your unique swag, women will take care of you, monetarily and physically. There are different swags men possess. For example, my father has the "*Romance Smooth Swag*" with a combination of the "*Luxury Dream Swag.*" Upon meeting women, he would attempt to romance them by making them feel like a queen. He would promise to give them the world, and once these promises are made, they would want to stay committed to him. This is a driven type of swag, but it comes with a dear price. For example, if a man does not meet his promises, he will lose that woman and she will be disappointed because he could not deliver on those promises.

One of my uncles has the "*All-American Polished Swag.*" Before he decided to fully commit, he was a complete ladies' man. With the All-American Polished Swag, you would chase success, and you should be a leader. With this swag, you would also stay sociable, and you should make sure that you dress nice. My uncle would demonstrate this swag by joining a known college fraternity; he would take luxury trips; he would purchase cars that attract women, and he would purchase fine linens that would help him stay attractive. While being a ladies' man, his vehicle was always polished, inside and out!! This type of swag breaths success and dominance, and women love this swag because it is very polished.

Some men have the "*Presidential Swag*" or the "*Self-Confidence Swag.*" With these swags, a man has the traits of a leader, and he has a since of confidence about himself. He is a very hard worker, and he believes he can accomplish anything he puts his mind to. This is a driven swag, and women love this man because of his confidence and drive. This swag turns a woman on because a man who has this swag is usually very established. He also attempts to wear the finest linens. If a woman gets this man, she feels as if she has a winner because this man has to win, and he is very competitive. He competes at all costs and he has to be successful; whether it's being successful at buying a home, buying a car, getting a promotion at his job, or owning his own business, he has to win!!! When a man is a winner, he is usually successful, and women flock to success.

Then, there is the "*Hustler-Swag*" or the "*Gangster Swag.*" With the Hustler Swag or the Gangster Swag, a man appears to be the complete Hustler. He makes a lot of money, and he usually search for ways to purchase luxury items. He also knows the streets, and he doesn't mind taking illegal risks to make his ends meet. This man tends to drive the nicest cars, wear the finest linens and he attracts a lot of women. With this swag, women are attracted to this man because they like his lifestyle, as well as the material things that he has acquired. This man's lifestyle is usually flashy, and women want to be part of his flashiness. They would flock to him because of the material things he possesses. These types of men usually attract Gold Digging woman.

Each and every man should have his unique swag. It all depends on the individual and his lifestyle. For example, my womanizer friend of 20 years has the "***Pretty boy—Playboy Swag.***" He constantly expresses that he has mastered his swag. Every time he talks to a woman he believes he can sleep with her. With this swag, he keeps a clean shave and a clean haircut, and he would purchase the most expensive shoes on the market; weather its sneakers are dress shoes. With this swag, he tries to purchase the finest cologne, and he would attempt to wear the finest linens, such as polo shirts or designer jeans. Although this swagger may be very expensive, it pays off because women will flock to your success or your perceived success.

If a man considers himself a humorous individual, he usually possesses the Humorous Swag. If you possess this type of swag, it's important to capitalize on this "***Humorous Swag.***" Women love a man who is funny and can make them laugh. This man can entertain women for hours, and they will always want to have conversations with this type of man because they think he is hilarious. Men who contain the humorous swag should capitalize on their God given talent, but it is important to understand that sometimes you have to draw the line with your humor. Being overly silly or overly humorous may turn a woman off; so it is necessary to show a serious side when necessary.

Then, there is the "***Dirty Boy Swag.***" Men who possess this swag always never appear to be well-groomed. As strange as it may sound, women may be attracted to this type of man. This man may have a 70's style with a since of relaxation, or he may look like a street thug. This man may wear T-Shirts and Khaki slacks, and he is not concerned about the latest fashions. With this swag, this man may also wear dingy jeans and dingy shirts. He would usually wear his hair long, and he occasionally shaves his face. Although this swag is called, the Dirty Boy Swag, this man walks and talks with a lot of confidence, and some women are usually tuned on by his uniqueness.

Like men, women can be shallow creatures. Some women will focus on the man's success or his swag, and she will commit to him because of the type of car he drives or other materialistic things he has accumulated throughout his life. For example, when men obtain advance educational degrees, women may commit to them. A woman would also commit to a man who belongs to a social group, such as fraternities, etc. Men, whether you are married or single, to get women to stay attracted to you and fully commit, you have to determine your swag; capitalize on your uniqueness and always keep a since of confidence about yourself.

Supporter

When it comes to making a woman commit, men, we need to start listening to our women!! Listening and supporting our women is essential when attempting to make them commit. Women are communicators, and they love to talk. They are very emotional creatures, and listening to their problems will make them feel special. When a woman talks, it may be necessary to act like you are paying attention to them, although you do not care about what they are talking about, for the meantime, you should act like you care. If you do this, it would take you far in your relationship. You should always remember: never come off as you are not interested in her conversations. A woman wants a friend, and she will make love to her friend quicker than she will make love to a complete stranger. So, you must establish a friendship or an emotional bond with a woman if you ever want them to commit. We should support our women because they are emotional creatures and they may need a man's help when things get tough. Men, there is a thin line when it comes to listening and becoming a woman's friend. While becoming her friend, we need to make sure that we do not to fall in the dreaded "Friend Zone." This concept would be discussed later in this book.

Provider/ Head of Household

Men, we should be providers. If a woman makes more money than you, you should stay secure about your financial situation and continue to be the head of your household. In a capitalist society, even in a recession, a man can find some type of employment. Upon losing a job, the worst thing you can do is fall into a depressed financial state of mind. Being a provider can cause a lot of stress, but it's important to understand that in the world we live in, individuals can start their own company and be successful at any type of endeavor. A man with an able body can attend school, start a business, work as a labor, gain a skill or obtain a trade. All these things will bring success to a man's life. Real men practice chasing success by staying focus on their career goals, and a Real man constantly attempts to improve himself. Men, we should never be lazy because a lazy man will never prosper. Women flock to a man who is driven. If a man has a lawn care service, he attends school, he works as a roofer, and he also works part-time as a package handler; he will have a nice car because he needs to go to work. This man will also have a home because he needs a place to lay his head after he works hard from one of his jobs. We should always have a chip on our shoulders when it comes to making money and becoming a provider, but we shouldn't boast or brag about our efforts or our accomplishments. The hard work should be effortless.

There is a very important verse in the Bible that explains how a man should not fall victim to "Laziness." According to the Book of Proverbs, Solomon son of David, King of Israel, was considered one of the wisest men whom ever lived on Earth. In this book he stated: "I walked by the field of a lazy person, the vineyard of one with no common sense. I saw that it was overgrown with nettles. It was covered with weeds, and its walls were broken down. Then, as I looked and thought about it, I learned this lesson: a little extra sleep, a little more slumber, a little folding of the hands to rest, then **POVERTY** will pounce on you like a **BANDIT**; **SCARCITY** will attack you like an armed robber." (Proverbs 24: 30-34) Basically, this scripture explains how a lazy man fail to harvest his garden, and weeds started to grow. This scripture directly applies to a man's life, and men should work hard to overcome laziness. When a man sleeps all the time and he continues to slumber, he will be forced into poverty. On Earth, there are limited resources to man, whether it is land or food, these resources are scarce and they will always be scarce. So, men, it takes hard work, dedication and commitment to obtain these scarce resources on Earth, but if we diligently work and never fall victim to laziness, we will never have a problem making a woman commit.

Pride/ Stand up to a Challenge

Men, although we need swag, we should try to let our woman know that we do not have too much pride; basically, you should have a since of confidence, but you should not be a chauvinist. There is a balance when it comes to having pride and having too much pride. We need to show a woman that we can handle any challenge that comes our way, but in the midst of things, we should be very humble. For example, we can talk about how we can dominate in a sport, but at the same time, we should make it aware that we still need improvement. As men, we should not complain about our lively situations and problems. If we do talk about our problems, we should talk about how to create solutions for our problems. When this happens, women will support us and they will attempt to help us reach your goals.

Think like a Man, and Not like a Boy

If God is in our life, there is nothing that we cannot do or accomplish. A "Real Man," does not think like a boy, and he doesn't need friends to dictate to him when and how he should make his money or how he should provide for his family. A "Real Man" doesn't need anyone to validate his social well-being. For the "Real Man," God is the only source that validates how he conducts his life. As men, we fall into a trap of thinking that we have to please the "boys," or our so called "friends." Some men neglect their woman and their family because they want to please their so called friends. A man should never think like a boy, and therefore he should never let another man dictate to him how he should provide for his family. Although, it is important to socialize with other male counterparts, you should let your friends know their place when it comes to your household. We can make one of the most dreaded mistakes by making our friends priority instead of putting our immediate family first. When a "Real Man" provides for his family, a woman will have a great deal of respect for him. If your so called friend disrespects your kids, and your woman, he is not your friend because he should respect you as a man as well as respect your family.

Men, you must remember, success along with charm turns a woman on. You should capitalize on your swag and have a since of confidence. ***It's also important to remember: A woman will never chase a man who never chases money.*** So, you as a man should never stop chasing money if you ever want a woman to commit.

CHAPTER 4—MY WANTS AND MY NEEDS
(Woman's guide to make him commit)

I drop down to my knees and I plead one of my most desperate needs.
My need to love you; this is what I want, to touch you; thinking of kissing you.
These are my wants and my needs; thinking how you are a necessity.

Being close to you, just to have one touch,
your love continue to be what I want. This is what, I think I need,
but are you a true necessity?
As I plead; for the need, thinking how you may be the one who will bear my seed.

Is love what I need? Are you what I want, but I ask, are you what I need?
Trying to prove *this*, deep *hypothesis*;
will you help me to strive, will you be my helper, as I provide?
Will you take my lead; can I be what you need?

These needs and wants are my burning desires,
there's no secret that you take me higher, as you continue to be the one I admire.

I can see the pureness of your heart; how can we ever be apart?
Understanding, that *you* also have needs.
The need for a real man; the need to let you know,
that I can do all that which no other man can.

Please, let me, let you see, how I can actually,
prove that you are the one and only.
Together, you and I *can* have it *all*; several luxuries,

extravagant wonderful means; receiving what this world has to give,
as we continue to live.

I know that you are here to help motivate me;
that's why when I have the opportunity,
I try to prove that you are my destiny; more than just a necessity.
You are pure as waking up to a sunny day; this is why I pray that you will always
stay.

My wishes and my desires will one day all come true,
I want to prove, that *you* need me as much as I need you!!!

My Wants and My Needs

THE EXPLANATION = THE INTERPRETATION: MY WANTS AND MY NEEDS

In this poetic piece, it explains want a man want when he pursues a woman. This piece expresses how the man in this poem holds back his feelings of being in love, but deep down he is truly in love. This piece also expresses how he perceives his woman. When reading this poem, it's important to understand the meaning of a necessity. A necessity is not a want, it's a need. For example, we need water and food to survive, and this poem states that a woman should be a necessity. Ladies, when a man sees you as a necessity, he will fully commit to you. When it comes to relationships, men can be very indecisive, and this is seen in this poetic piece. The man in this poem is unsure about his relationship because he is uncertain about his woman's values. Men are always in pursuit for a woman who is his ideal type and she must love him unconditionally.

Equally Yoked

Ladies, men desire to be loved, but there are several reasons why we may not want to commit. When a woman wants a man to commit, she must learn her man. She must find out what he really wants. This may be a challenging task, but it can be done. Men are always in pursuit of the right woman, and if a woman is not **equally yoked** with us, it would be difficult for us to commit. While in pursuit of the ideal woman, a man will date multiple women until he finds his true soul mate. Men seem to commit to a woman if he thinks another man wants her, especially when she has it going on!! For example, if you dress nice, keep your hair done, pamper yourself, keep your toes done, pursue your career and stay "**JAZZY**," it will be easy for you to attract men. Ladies, being jazzy is the woman's version of a man's Swag. So, when you have self-confidence, and you have a sexy jazzy demeanor, men will approach you and they will want to commit to you, but being overly jazzy will make you seem stuck up, and no man wants a stuck up woman. Being stuck up and overly confident will instantly turn men off. So, it's best to find a balance when it comes to being jazzy and confident.

All men are not the same, but most men value a woman who is submissive, with a since of independence. Ladies, men love women who are unique with their own touch of jazziness. We also want a woman who has a positive attitude. For example, if a woman's attitude is nasty, we would be very slow to commit. Men value respectable women, and if you have our value system, we would keep you around and eventually marry you. A man can value different things about a woman. Some men may value a woman who attends church, a woman who is trendy, a woman who loves to have sex, or a woman who likes sports. Men usually do not value women who have a very controlling demeanor. A woman who has a controlling demeanor usually aggravates a man. Men usually do not like a woman who disrespects him by calling him derogatory names. If a woman degrades him, he might be very slow to commit. A man will only sleep with a disrespectful woman, but once he no longer wants her sex, he will leave her alone.

Most men want a woman who works hard and who will be a great mother by teaching his kids positive values. As a lady, it's also important to know that cleanliness is essential when it comes to making a man commit. We love women who know how to keep a clean house, and we love a woman who likes to clean. If a woman is nasty and unclean, it says a lot about her. For example, if a man visits your house, and you have dirty laundry and dirty dishes every time he comes over; he would think twice about committing to you.

Ladies, if a man does not have a spiritual connection with you, he may also question his desires for you. **Spiritual Love** is very important for both a man and a woman. Spiritual Love is when two souls come together, to make one. With Spiritual Love, both the man and the woman desire each other and it will be difficult for them to live without one another. Being spiritually connected means that the couple is equally yoked. Most men want a woman who is God fearing, but she must have a complete balance of spiritual life and natural life. Although a man may want a woman who is God fearing, she can't be over religious or judgmental when it comes his bad habits. When you always point out a man's wrong doings, it may force him not to fully commit. Ladies, when your man has bad habits, you should encourage him to get rid of his bad habits instead of preaching to him about his bad habits. When it comes to his mishaps, you should **talk with him, and don't talk to him**. It's important to be honest with him and let him know that some of his bad habits can't be tolerated. If he really wants to be with you, he will take every measure to get rid of his bad habits, or he would tailor his bad habits to suit your needs. As a woman, you should make a decision and ask yourself, "do you want to deal with his bad habits, or do you want to leave him?" If you constantly nag him, it's never a good thing. It is best to pray for him, and let God enter his life and wait until God make him fully change. If you discuss leaving him because of his bad habits, it's important to gracefully let him know that you want to leave because of his bad habits. When this happens, if he really wants to be with you, he will at least attempt to change, and in the mist of his change, he would start to show a true commitment.

In this poem, the man questions his love for the woman who he is currently dating because he is fresh out of a previous relationship. When a man is fresh out of a serious relationship, he might need time to heal. It usually takes men two years to fully move on from their previous relationships. The worst thing a woman can do when a man is fresh out of a serious relationship is: Pressure him to quickly enter into a new one. If he is only looking for a friendship, it's important to just be friends. You should control your emotions when you are just friends with him, and on frequent occasions, you should re-iterate your friendship with him. When this happens, he will think twice about putting you off. Ladies, if you tell him that you have other male friends, you should be very discrete about it because you do not want to appear to be promiscuous. When women are promiscuous, men usually will not take them serious. However, it's important to know, if you are dating multiple men, place your phone on silent when you are out on a date with him. While on a date, you should slightly talk about other men who pursue you, but you should remember to be very discrete about speaking about these other men. You should never over indulge in deep conversations about past relationships, but you should slightly let him know how guys pursue you. Once this happens, you would get commitment points.

Getting out of his "Friend Zone"

Men and women think differently, and a man can sleep with a woman for years with no emotional attachment. There are several reasons why a man may put a woman in his Friend Zone. He may keep you in the Friend Zone because he may think you are overweight, very promiscuous or he thinks you are not equally yoked with him. If you want to get out of his Friend Zone, you must cut off the sex or you should slow down on the sexual encounters. Once the sex stops or decreases, he will stop seeing you and you can find someone who truly wants to be with you. Also, if you want to get out of his Friend Zone, first you should ask him, "Do you ever see us in a relationship?" If he says something like, "maybe, but he really doesn't know at the current time," you have a chance. It's best to not revisit this same question, and listen to his reasons why he is not ready for a full committed relationship. If he gives you a bazzar answer to your commitment question, you may want to leave him along because you will never get out of his Friend Zone. If you ask him, "Do you see us as a couple?" and he says something like: "no, you are not my type;" you just might not be his type!! Most women get confused by this answer because he may sleep with you for years, but as men, we may love the sex, but not love the woman. We can commit to the sexual relationship, but we may never want to commit to the relationship. It might be several reasons why we will not commit to the relationship. Ladies, as mentioned earlier, we may not like your attitude, or we may think that you are overweight, or you may not be equally yoked with us. We might think that you don't value our value system and when this happens, we will keep you in our "Friend Zone," but we will stay committed to the sex.

Women, when you are in a man's Friend Zone, it's important to benefit from being friends with benefits. Ladies, when you are in his Friend Zone, you should play it cool. You should focus more on yourself.

You shouldn't look for anything more than just a friendship, and you should benefit from the sex and the good times that comes along with being friends with benefits. Ladies, when you find a new man, you should communicate with the "Friends with Benefits" man and let him know that you have found someone else, and you no longer want to sleep with him. Although he may be a little upset, he will respect your decision and he would attempt to leave you alone. Remember, he will attempt to leave you alone, but he will constantly pursue you for sex. You should cut him off because he will be wasting your time.

The second way to get out of a man's Friend Zone is: you should not make yourself readily available. If he says, "I have a lot of things going on, and maybe there will be a possibility that I will commit," the best thing for you to do is: wait it out and see how things goes, but you should never stress about being more than just friends. If he is not moving fast enough for you, it's best to leave him alone, and move on. During his Friend Zone, you should find ways to preoccupy your time. You should not place extra emphasis on him because the feelings are not mutual. When you are with him, you should discuss with him how good of a friend he is, and you should not pressure a commitment. Ladies, although you want more in the relationship, you should frequently bring up how you want the relationship to be more; you should flirt with the suggestion, but never over do it because it will push him away. To be more than friends, you must act like you don't want more than just a friendship. This may sound strange, but it works!!! One day, he will say, "I want you to be my woman," and it will be a total surprise. Ladies it works like this: if he really wants you, and enjoy your sex, you should stay calm, live your life and if he doesn't capitalize on his opportunities to have you, you should make him realize that he has missed out on a good thing!!! When you find someone else, you shouldn't think twice about moving on. Enjoy passionate sex with your new man, and let him reap all of the benefits of you being his woman.

Ladies, remember a man might place you in his Friend Zone because of his current state of mind or his current financial situation. Placing you in his Friend Zone does not mean that you are not is ideal type of woman. Men like to be financially secure before they fully commit to a woman, especially if the woman he is dating values nice things. Although each and every man is different, for most men, if a man express that his finances are not where he expects them to be, it will be difficult for him to focus on a relationship. If pressured to be in a relationship, and his financial situation is not right, he may lash out to you. He may abuse you verbally or physically, so it's best to let him come around, and you should ease out of his Friend Zone with no added pressures.

If he is working to improve his financial situation, as a woman, you should respect his decision to not enter a fully committed relationship. When a man makes it clear, that being equally yoked is not the problem, as a woman, it's important to be true to yourself and decide if you want to wait on this man, or move on. If you can wait on him to get himself together, he will appreciate your sacrifice. This wait-it-out period may be three to six months. When a man loses his job, he is entitled to unemployment benefits for 6 months, and if an employer can wait 6 months for a person to get back on his or her feet and obtain another job, you should be willing to wait-it-out for 6 months for the man you want to get his self together. In this situation, ladies, don't be afraid to ask him to give you an estimate time when he might be ready for a fully commit relationship because you don't want to keep revisiting this question. When it comes to commitment, every man has a different time frame, and it might be 2 months or up to 6 months to fully commit. But if he is fresh out of a serious relationship, such as a previous engagement or a marriage, it may take him up to 2 years for him to full commit again. The man's Friend Zone is different from a woman's Friend Zone because a man will attempt to make a woman feel good about herself by sexually satisfying her. If you are in his Friend Zone, wait it out, but if you can't wait, be honest with yourself and walk away from the relationship, and most of all, decline his sexual favors. If you do this, you will get out of his Friend Zone!!

Promiscuous

In this poem, the man questions his love for that woman and his desires to provide for that woman. Ladies, in this poetic piece, it expresses, "The need for a Real Man; the need to let you know, that I can do all that which no other man can." As men, we are competitive by nature, and we desire our woman to not show a promiscuous side. Although, every woman has a past, as a woman, you should not express every sexual act or every sexual encounter that you have experienced when you have dated previous men. Ladies, if you have slept with several men, you should keep your details discrete by telling just a few things about your sexual past. You don't have to tell him every sexual encounter that you have had in the past. If you tell these types of things, it will be difficult for him to fully commit to you because he may see you as a very promiscuous woman. It may be fine to discuss a sexual encounter with another woman because he may find it sexy that you have a sexual wild side. He might find it exotic that you may be open to invite another woman to your bedroom. Most men fantasize about being with two women at the same time, but if you express how you had a threesome with two men; he may perceive you to be a slut. Ladies, this is just how it is!!

Her Wants and her Desires

Women make terrible mistakes by placing unwanted pressures on men. Women will stay in pursuit of the perfect man, but when this man never arrives, she will stay single. Ladies, instead of being with the perfect man, you can work with that man, and you can help motivate him to stay driven. If he can measure up to your basic needs, you should give him a chance. Ladies when you give these men a chance, you would be surprised because that man will show you a very good time, and you may even find yourself falling in love with him. If a man has the basic needs, such as a job, a nice personality, a car and his own place, you should at least give him a chance to get to know you. Sometimes women place men under a lot of pressure, and when that man gets fed up with that woman, she is once again single and alone. Ladies, I am not saying that you should completely lower your standards, but if a man has goals, and he treats you right, and he doesn't overwhelm you with his financial burdens, it's important to give that man a chance.

Men and women make mistakes when it comes to dating. A man may want the super model chic, and he may pass up on the average looking woman and in the midst of things, he misses out on a good thing. Likewise, women make the major mistake by pursuing the "Perfect Man." A woman might be in pursuit of a man who makes more than $75,000 dollars on a yearly basis. A woman might also want a man who has no children, or a man who has a college degree, or a man who has a 750+ credit score, but women should realize, although a man may not be perfect, he may still be an awesome man!! Women, if you give him a chance and date him, you will find out that he makes a decent living, he may be a good father to his kids, and you may find that you can work around his credit. Once you give him a chance, you will notice that this man can be your true soul-mate. When dating and searching for the ideal mate, if the values and goals are there, you would be surprised when you find out how wonderful this man can be. The professional woman will usually find herself single because her standards are too high, and when men notice that her standards are set too high, the man she dates will find ways to leave her alone, eventually never showing a true commitment.

Overly Anxious & Jealous

If that man expresses that he is not ready to show a commitment, you should never seem needy or overly anxious to be with him. Women make the major mistake by chasing a man who doesn't want her. If you desire a man, it's important to pursue him for a while, but if he doesn't show a true interest, you should not continue to pursue him because you will appear to be desperate and thirsty. For example, if a man or a woman goes for a job interview, that person should never show that they are desperate for a job. Once a person seems desperate for a job, that person looses value in their worth. This simple concept applies to a woman while dating men. Ladies, when you seem overly anxious, you appear to have a lesser value. If you seem overly anxious to get in a relationship with that man, that man will be very slow to commit.

Again, to get a man to commit, you should be patient and don't force him to commit. Not forcing him to commit makes him want to commit. It is a simple concept: you should focus on improving your-self worth. Ladies, you should not keep repeating how desirable you are, it's important to **SHOW** how desirable you are because actions speak louder than words!!! You should grow spiritually, independently and physically. Doing these things will surely make him come around and show a true commitment. *Ladies, you should stay desirable to other men, and when this happens, you will make the man you want, desperately want you.*

If a woman is overly jealous, this may stop a man from committing. If you constantly check his phone, or if you constantly harass him about his past relationships, or if you have trust issues, he may question if he want to commit to you. The overly jealous category also relates to your jealous friends. If you have friends that are always interfering with your relationship, a man will be very slow to commit. You should understand where to draw the line when it comes to your friends and your relationship. If your friends always try to influence you to leave your man, you should respect your friend's opinion, but it's your call if you want to rely on her opinion or not. Ladies, you should remember to decipher good opinions from bad opinions. When it comes to your friends, you have to be very discrete when it comes to their opinion because misery always loves company. If your friends are single, they may also want you to be single.

Woman's Weight

In this poem, the man again questions his love for this woman; he may question his love because of her weight. If a man is not attracted to your weight and size, he may question his desires for you. Ladies, yes, weight can be a very sensitive topic, but for men, a woman's weight does matter!! Men are visual creatures, and although weight may not be a true deciding factor in a man's decision to fully commit, it does play a factor. Ladies, it works like this; a woman would not prefer a broke, drunk lazy man, and a man would not prefer a broke, lazy fat woman. There are some men who love big girls, and if you are a big girl, you should be proud of your big girl status. Men love a healthy, confident big girl who knows she is sexy. If you are a big girl, the worst thing you can do is look down on your big girl status. If you are not confident and love yourself, how can you get a man to love you? If you are a big girl, you should always walk sexy and talk sexy. If a man doesn't like it, it's best that he leave you alone and you should let him find him a skinny girl who can better suit his needs.

If you are not sure about your man wanting to commit because you're not his ideal weight, you should have a discussion with him and ask him and ask him, "how does he feel about you losing a couple of pounds?" If he gives an over joyous reaction, and he suggests that you should go to the gym more often, you should consider losing weight. When it comes to a woman's weight, men usually reject women with a severe case of "**Booty-Do**." Booty-Do is a term men use to explain when a woman's stomach sticks out more than their Booty-Do. A bad case of Booty-Do may turn a man off. Although men may not admit it, a server case of Booty-Do is a major concern. He may not mention your Booty-Do because if he mentions it, you may feel uncomfortable. If you know that you have Booty-Do, it's important to have frequent conversations with your man about how you workout at your local gym. You should also let him know that you are attempting to lose your Booty-Do. If he thinks you have a severe case Booty-Do, he will be slow to commit, especially if you are a small petite woman. Ladies, men will give you a pass if you have Booty-Do because you just had a baby, but if your baby is 3 years old and you claim to have Booty-Doo because of your baby, that man might think that you are making excuses for not being active in your local gym. Ladies, remember if you happen to have Booty-Doo, you should never be insecure. You should try to stay focus and work to improve your overall look. When it comes to weight, you should attempt to stay healthy for yourself, and you shouldn't lose weight for the sake of a man. If you are a plus size woman, and you enjoy being plus size, you should stay patient and let God send you a man who like plus size women. There are a lot of men who adore full figured, plus size women. When plus size women are confident and have a sexy demeanor about themselves, it's very easy for them to attract a man.

Due to the fact that men are very visual creatures, we visualize how a woman will look after she bears our child. This is stated in the poem, "As I plead; for the need, thinking how you may be the one who will bear my seed." A woman must communicate with that man and let him know that she will be committed to stay fit after she bears his child. Some men tend to visualize what a woman would look like in 20 years. Upon meeting the woman's mother, men will be a little stagnant about his commitment if a woman's mother is not the ideal weight and size. If your mother is severely overweight, or he sees one of your female family members who are severely overweight, he may have doubts about committing to you. He will question: "will you meet his wants and needs by keeping a tasteful figure well into the future, or will you let yourself go and gain 40, 50 or 60 pounds?" Ladies, this is just how it is. Although this may sound weird, men have shallow visual ways, but its best to let him know that you will not let yourself go if he happens to meet one of your family members who are slightly overweight.

Emotional Intelligence

Women should learn how to control their emotions. When a woman is extra dramatic and extra emotional, a man may think that this woman maybe crazy. Men usually perceive these women as "Drama Keepers." Men are simple and sometimes we will act as if we do not hear you when you attempt to get your point across, but we are quite because we are simple. We don't like to argue or talk about certain situations at certain times. We might be in our moment of relaxation.

The extra emotional woman will always need a hug; she is always in need to be recognized when he comes into the house, and/or she nags about any and everything that bothers her in the relationship. When a man comes home from work, he sometimes need at least 30 minutes to an hour before he wants to hear about taking out the trash or answering questions about a your weight, etc. Ladies, you should learn how to control your emotions if you want a man to commit. You should practice, emotional intelligence. With emotional intelligence, a woman understands how to control her emotions. A woman who understands emotional intelligence will never throw things at their man when she gets upset. In an argument, women should NEVER say things that would be difficult to take back. Doing an argument, women can be very cruel. A woman can say things that will hurt a man deeply. For example, during an argument, a woman can tell a man that his penis is too small and that's why she slept with his best friend. During a heated argument, a woman may also tell a man that because he loves his dog, he chooses his dog over his children. Although a man may love his dog, he will never choose his dog over his kids. Women, when you want to discuss an important matter in the relationship, it's important to ask, "When is it a good time to talk?" Bedtime might be a good time, or over dinner may be a great time to discuss things that may be on your mind. When a woman nags a man, she runs him off, making it hard for him to commit or stay committed.

Your Kids

First and foremost, if a man does not accept your kids, it's best to reconsider your relationship with him. When you have kids, and he doesn't accept your kids, there may be problems in the relationship, especially if your kids are under the age of 10. If a man has problems with your children, it's not worth placing him before your kids. Women, while dating, every man does not need to meet your children. There isn't a time frame for meeting kids, but it's recommended that you wait at least a month before he meets your children. While dating, its best that you get to know him before your kids get to know him. When dating, it's best to let a man know that you and your kids are a package deal. Some men can't deal with women with children, and once this is known, it's best to let him find a woman who doesn't have kids. When it comes to kids, men always like women to be straight forward, and most men would instantly let you know if they have a problem with kids. For example, if he doesn't like you because you have kids, he may give you a cold shoulder, or he may complain about other people's kids. When this happens, it's best to ask him if your kids bother him. If he gives you an answer that isn't straight forward, you may want to reconsider your relationship with him.

Ladies, but on the flip side of things, if you notice that this man does like kids, he may want to be a father figure to your kids. There are some men who will only date women who have kids because these men want or desire to be a father figure. Kids are a blessing, and once a man and your children develop a good relationship, he will show a better commitment to you. This man will start to take on the daddy role, and as a woman, you will see him commit because not only will he love you, he will also love your kids.

His Issues

In this poem, again the man questions his love and desires for that woman. Men may be stagnant to commit if they are not financially stable. For some men, it's important to be able to financially cater to a woman, as well as be a provider for his family. When men do not have the means to financially provide, we may be very slow to commit. To improve our financial state, we may work several jobs, and we may not have time to be in a fully committed relationship. In troublesome financial situations, we may want to stay focus on getting ourselves together before committing. Ladies, it's important that you let us have the necessary space we need when we try to improve our financial situation.

Men tend to seek a woman who will be a Helper, a Motivator and not a Dictator. When women start to dictate, and not help and motivate, they usually push a man away. Dictating to him makes him feel less than a man. If his finances are not intact, he may hold back his feelings for you. This is expressed in the poem, "together, you and I can have it all; several luxuries, extravagant wonderful means; receiving what this world has to give, as we continue to live." A man always wants to feel like a man. He never wants to appear as if he cannot give his woman all that she financially desires. If a man's career is unstable, he may tend to hold back, but if that woman communicate with him and express how she will be by his side, no matter what his financial situation, he will start to show a full commitment to her. He will stop doubting if his woman is right for him. A man always wants to know, will a woman stick by his side, during the tough times and the good times.

Why men take on the "Baby Daddy Role"

As stated in this poem, "My wants and My needs," as men, we have wants and needs to have a family. Ladies, we tend to want to start a family, but if our financial situation is not intact, we would hold back and not fully commit. This is displayed in the line of the poem that says: "As I plead; for the need, thinking how you may be the one who will bear my seed." Some men may want a woman to have his kids, but we may question the need to fully commit if our career is not stable or if we do not have the means to fully provide for our child. A man may get you pregnant, and decide that the pregnancy was not the right option for him because of his finances, and when you decide not to terminate the pregnancy and you decide to keep the child, some men, not ALL men, take on the **"Baby Daddy"** role. Again, when men father a child because of the want of becoming a father, but he does not have the financial means to take care of the child, he may take on the "Baby Daddy" role.

Some men may get you pregnant, and he will use the pregnancy to trap you, thinking that if you have has his kids, you will not leave him. When this happens, he doesn't want to be a father, he just wants to be a "Baby Daddy."

The Pregnancy Trap: "The Ole Keep a Brother Baby" baby daddy role continued . . .

Men will also take on the "Baby Daddy" role when he thinks that you all are not equally yoked. You may not have the ideal weight, looks, the ideal job, etc. Women make a major mistake by assuming that, if you have his baby, he will commit to you. In fact, if he thinks you got pregnant in hopes to make him commit, instead of committing, he may never want to commit. He would eventually taking on the Baby Daddy role.

In some cases, being a Baby Daddy doesn't mean that he will not provide for that child. He may not want you, but he may choose to be in his child's life from a distance. If he does not want to provide for his child, you may have to pursue a court order to make him pay child support, but ladies, if he attempts to take care of his kids, you **SHOULD NOT** pursue a child support order, especially if you want him back into your life. You all should work on becoming a family and take care of the baby together. If he feels as if you use the court order to make him upset, he may see you as being vindictive, and he may never want commit to you. You should not worry when a man does not want to commit, and he decides to take on the Baby Daddy role. The best thing to do when he adopts the Baby Daddy role is to accept that he is just your child's father. If he doesn't want to be with you, your only concern should be to take care of your child.

To conclude this section, this poem also explains how the man desires to have a family with the woman who he thinks he loves. The line, "you may be the one who will bear my seed," also means that this man wants to start a family. For men, love can be very complicated at times because we are in pursuit of finding someone who is equally yoked. Also, in this poem, the man asks the question: "is she my ideal soul mate?" This is explained by the line in the poem, "I can see the pureness of your heart, and how can we ever be apart?" This poem also explains how this man may want to start a life with this woman. This poetic piece also expresses the need to have such a person in his life that motivates him on a daily basis, and this poem ends with the deep question: "Can I prove to you that I can be what you need?" Although there are several reasons men will not commit, it's important to believe in yourself, focus on self improvement, learn what he seeks in a woman, and be very patient and you will see a commitment. You should always be true to yourself, and if he is not moving fast enough, you should never hesitate to move on. You should also patiently wait for that ideal man to walk into your life.

SECTION II

The Chasing Game—*The cheating man, temptation, avoiding her Friend Zone*

While you SCREAM at your woman, there's a man wishing he could talk softly to her ear.
While you HUMILIATE, OFFEND and INSULT her, there's a man flirting with her and reminding her how wonderful she is.
While you HURT your woman, there's a man wishing he could make LOVE to her.
While you make your women CRY there's a man Stealing smiles from her.

-Anonymous

CHAPTER 5—WHY DO I CHEAT?

(Women's guide as to why he cheats)

Is my Flesh weak, I don't know, but I have to creep.
The feeling is so good; my other woman makes love to me like she should.
To cheat, my main women always say: I wish you would!!

What happens when she finds out; that I am something like a disguise,
with all of my lies; this cheating, I have to hide,
but I am determined to make my main relationship stay alive.

She can't find out that I have multiple chicks;
this cheating makes me feel like a character in a motion action flick.
I am a Star, and with Facebook and Twitter, I can love all of them from a Far.

Why must I womanize, is it the big breasts, and the sexy thighs,
or is it because I have the Lustful eye?

These flings started as a simple flirt. Asking why must I chase the skirt?
I even chase it at work!!

It's never my fought; I will continue until I get caught.
Some of these women can even be bought;
Not with money, but with time, charm and romance; *Yes they can*;
I can even make them cheat on their man.

Why must I womanize, is it because I have the Lustful eye, attracted to the big
butts and the sexy thighs?

With this movie script, I give tips, compliments flowing from my lips.
I am the lead character, because I understand her;
Although it's more than two, or even a few; I tell her, that I only love you.
Damn she doesn't have clue, only if she really knew.

Don't judge me; because it's the feeling of a conquest,
trying to see if I can get them to all undress, it's simply a battle with my flesh.
It's wrong, but I try **not** to cheat, even thinking of cheating while in-between the
sheets, but again and again, I continue to creep.

They can't stop knocking at my door, calling my cell phone because they want more.
Truly, they are not what I am looking for; it's only one-who I adore.

These women all desire a good man, but its only one of me; I confess I am freak,
With my multiple sexual treats. It's not me; it's the flesh that's weak!!

I am sorry. If you give me, one more time; this is for my main dime. I will get it
right, as I drop down to one knee; I pray that you will understand me;
Although I cheat, I walk away, and don't cheat; but it's not me, it's my flesh that's weak.

That's Why I Cheat!!!

THE EXPLANATION = THE INTERPRETATION: WHY I CHEAT / WHY MEN CHEAT

This chapter introduces the cheating man. Although this chapter list reasons why men cheat, men cheat for different reasons. In this chapter, the strategies of a cheating man are also mentioned. The cheating man may possess multiple traits. For example, he might cheat because he is on a conquest to sleep with as many women as he can, or he might cheat because he has low-self-esteem. The cheating man might cheat because he wants approval from his male counterparts, or he may cheat because he enjoys having a roster full of women. He may also cheat because he can't control his sexual desires. These men always try to find a way out of a committed relationship, and this section tells how to spot a cheating man. Although this poetic piece has a comical feel, it has a lot of truth to it.

For the experienced cheating man, once he meets a woman, and after a couple of conversations with her, he knows if wants to have a relationship with her or not. If the cheating man thinks a woman is promiscuous or very gullible, he would try to sleep with her very quickly, and once he gets what he wants, he would move on to the next woman. If a woman dresses like a prostitute who advertises sex, that man would usually see this woman as a sex symbol and he would desperately try to sleep with her. During casual conversations, if a woman constantly talks about men she has been with in the past, the cheating man will would try his best to capitalize on the opportunity of sleeping with this woman. Ladies, when you constantly talk about men you have slept with in the past, the cheating man would patiently wait for his chance to have his big day with you.

The Conquest

Men have several ways of getting women to sleep with them, and for some men, sleeping with multiple women becomes a conquest. When a woman becomes part of a man's conquest and the sex is good, he would always want to have more sex with her and the sex will only come when it is convenient for him. If a woman has a nice body and a cute face, he will always brag to his friends about how he had the opportunity to sleep with her. The sexier she is, the more of an accomplishment it will be for him, especially if the woman doesn't come off to be easy or promiscuous. Men whom seek to conquer women do not care about a woman's career goals or her aspirations in life. These men are actors, and they usually put on a disguise. Ladies, these men act as if they are very interested in you until they get to know you and then they entice your mind. In the poetic piece, it states: "I am the main character because I understand her. Although it's one or two, or even a few, I tell her that I only love you. She doesn't have a clue, only if she really knew." This explains that this man is a character, and he tells a particular woman that he loves her because this is what she wants to hear. This poetic piece also states, "She can't find out that I have multiple chics, all of this cheating makes me feel like a character in a Motion Action Flick." This cheating man feels as if he is a famous porn star who can easily conquer women. This type of man enjoys lying, and he is an expert in the art of manipulation. This is stated in the verse: "she can't find out that I am something like a disguise, with all of my lies." This cheating man attempts to not get caught while he is on his conquest of sleeping with as many women as he possibly can.

For the conquering cheating man, once a woman opens her legs and gives him the sex, he has accomplished his conquest. This cheating man looks at woman as if they are a piece of meat, and although he treats you like a lady or a queen for the moment, this man is only interested in your physical pleasure. If he can get other things out of you, such as money, he would. Ladies, once again, once this cheating man achieves his goal of sleeping with you, he would move on to the next woman. He would continue to be on his journey of sleeping with as many women as he possibly can. Although this cheating man cheats, and he has reckless sexual behaviors, he would usually protect himself during sex. This man knows that he has multiple women, and there might be one woman whom he likes the best, and although he cheats, he doesn't want to catch any unwanted sexually transmitted diseases or have any unwanted pregnancies. The experienced cheating man understands this concept.

The Roster

When a man cheats, he would usually have a roster of women. For the cheating man, once a woman shows interest in him, that man will place this woman on his roster. For this very experienced cheating man, he might have a black book full of women and he may list their female characteristics. This black book has women in categories, and the cheating man would usually label his women accordingly. In his black book, he would rate the woman's conversation, her sex, as well as their overall rankings. For example, he would state her name, the time he meet her, if he had sex with her, or if he considers her to be crazy or not. If he hasn't slept with her yet, he would also rank the possibilities of getting the goods out of her. If there is a strong possibility that he will never get the goods out of her, he will scratch her name out of his black book because she is useless to him.

The man's black book lists women by names, their characteristics and their position on his roster. He operates his roster like a basketball coach. In basketball, there would always be a Superstar player, and with the cheating man and his roster, he would usually pick a woman who treat him the best and make her his Superstar. When a woman decides to slack in her sexual duties or in her other womanly duties, he would degrade her position and make her a regular player on his team. He may even send her to the bench until he thinks she is ready to be a star player on his team. The cheating man may have a woman who kisses and sucks his penis very well, and he may give this woman and name as well as make her a superstar. He may name her "**Super Head**" because of the way she licks or suck on his penis. He may also have another woman on his team who is a good girl with big breast that sexes him very well. He may name this woman "**Thunder Titties**." Men give women names because they do not want to form an emotional attachment to them. The cheating man will also have a starting lineup of women, and when that woman no longer sexes him like the other one does, he would send that woman to the bench, and make another woman part of his main rotation. Once she is in his main rotation, she is considered to be in the starting line-up.

His Peers

When it comes to cheating, a man's peers are his greatest supporters. Men gain a lot of respect when they sleep with attractive women at ease. Men are competitive creatures, and conquering woman can become a game. After a man sleeps with a certain woman, like women, men go back and talk to their friends and tell how good the sex was. Being a player makes the cheating man seem like he has the "gift of the gab," or he can sweet talk any woman out of her panties. Some men cheat on their women because they want to see if they can sleep with a particular woman, and boast to their friends about his accomplishments. Once he cheats, he may not have any intentions to be with the other woman because he just wants bragging rights. Men like to brag about sports and they like to brag about women that they have slept with. When men sleep with a lot of women, they gain a high social status amongst their peers.

Although these men talk about sleeping with many different women, when the cheating man talks about cheating, he also discusses that he uses a condom while he cheats. When men are considered to be players, they are praised amongst their friends when they use condoms. Although it may be cool to be a player, it is not cool to have unprotected sex with multiple women because once a man has several kids by different women, the man would usually have to pay child support, and when this happens, he may never gain complete financial freedom, and his peers never want to be in this position. When the cheating man has unprotected sex with different women, he not only has the risk of having kids by different women, but he may also run the risk of catching something that he cannot get rid of. If a woman is very promiscuous, and a cheating man decides to have sex with her, he would make sure he protects his self during sex. For the man's peers, it's never cool to have unprotected sex with a very promiscuous woman. If the cheating man doesn't protect his self during sex, and he tells his friends about the episode, he would lose cool points. For most men, unprotected sex is considered a risky behavior and to be a player, one must play the game right and use condoms when having sex with multiple women.

Self-Esteem

Low Self-Esteem also plays a major role as to Why Men Cheat. Some men need self assurance that tells them that they still have "IT." Men sometimes want to feel as if they are desired by other women. When things are not going as planned in a man's life, he would step out on his relationship just to see if he is desired by other women. A man likes to see themselves as leaders and conquers, and if men sleep with several women, he will seem like he is important. If a man loses his job or his woman say things that would make him feel less than a man, he might find comfort in another woman. Once he meets this other woman, he might lie about his relationship status, and he will sleep with this other woman to make him feel good about himself. Sex can be a drug, and just like any other drug, sex can be an escape for men. Drugs make people feel good about themselves and sex can also make people feel good. For the low-self-esteem man, sex with other women can be exciting, and it will make him feel very important. For the low-self-esteem man, sleeping with a new woman can be a challenge, but when a man with low self-esteem sleeps with a very attractive non-promiscuous woman, his self-esteem rises tremendously. Men with low self-esteem may seek different women for different pleasures. As mentioned in earlier sections of this book, men and woman are different, and men can sleep with a woman for years and don't have any emotional attachments.

The Flesh

In this poetic piece, it highly focuses on the flesh, and it ends with the man battling his flesh. In this poetic piece, the man states: "Although I cheat, I always walk away and don't cheat; it's not me, it's my flesh that weak, that's why I cheat." Basically, this man expresses his guilt for not controlling his flesh. He expresses, although he cheats, he never cheats and he walks away from cheating. In this poetic piece, this man admits that he cheats, but he cannot control his flesh. He is a true addict of sex. Ladies, not all men have cheating tendencies, but some men cheat because they cannot control their flesh. All men are not the same, and they may battle with cheating; sex is like any other addiction. The flesh can be hard to control, and like people turn to food or drugs for comfort, some men turn to sex for comfort. Men can be addicted to porn, strip clubs or the traditional fling. In the poem, it states: "Why must I womanize, is it the Big Breast or the Sexy Thighs or is it because I have the Lust of the Eye?" This simply means that for the cheating man, he battles with the physical attraction of a woman, and he Lusts after every woman he sees. There was a pastor who stated, God intended sex to be a good thing, but Satan uses Lust to tempt man to commit sexual acts with strangers.

Ladies, it's easy for men to get physically turned on by a woman. A man's sexually organs are located on the outside of his body, and as men, if we hug a very attractive woman, we can easily get turned on. Men are very visual creatures and some men lust factor can be very strong. Men get turned on very easily, and when a very attractive woman wears skimpy clothes, some men zero-in on all of her sexual parts. When it comes to the flesh, for some men, it can be very difficult to control their sexual hormones. For the cheating man who cannot control his flesh, he would cheat on his woman if he no longer is attractive to her. If his woman gained 20 pounds or so, he would most likely cheat on her. Again ladies, men are visual creatures and putting on 20 to 30 pounds could turn a man to cheat, although he would still be in love with you. This cheating man would want the best of both worlds; a woman whom he sleeps with and a woman whom he seeks for comfort.

She needs some "Get Right"

When a woman constantly degrade her man, or make him feel like a wimp, this man will search for a woman who will treat him like a king. Although men do not show it, men have feelings. Women can also hold out on the sex, and when this happens, he would most likely seek sex from another woman, causing him to cheat. The cheating man will find what he is looking for in another woman, and he may seek sexual comfort from that other woman, until he would be satisfied. A man will also cheat if he no longer finds his woman attractive. Sometimes, a woman can let herself go and gain weight or she may fail to beautify herself. Ladies, men are visual creatures, and when we no longer find you attractive, we may cheat with a woman who we think is pleasing to the eye. A man will also cheat because he may not approve of your attitude. Women can be very cruel, and you all can say mean things, and a man can only take so much until he decides to cheat on you. When he expresses that he doesn't approve of your tone or your attitude, and if you decline to change your attitude and tone, your man would eventually start to cheat.

A man usually wants his woman to see eye-to-eye when it comes to his "*Sexual Value System*." Ladies, men may have certain sexual values that are important to him, and if his woman doesn't want to honor his Sexual Value System, he would usually cheat on her. For example, if he values sex and his woman don't value sex, he would find sex elsewhere in hopes to have his woman adopt his sexual values. He would have a woman on the side that completely pleases him, but he would keep his main woman. This may sound odd because you may ask the question, "Why doesn't he just leave his main woman alone and go with the other woman?" Well, a man will try to wait-it-out in hopes of his main woman will change and adapt his sexual value system. He would wait to see if his main woman would change, but if no changes take place, eventually, the other woman will slowly migrate into his life. This cheating man will slowly give the other woman what she wants, a full committed relationship. To simply put it ladies, men call this: "**Some Get Right in Her Life**." This cheating man will stay around and cheat on his woman in hopes that she changes for the better, but if she doesn't change, he will continue to cheat, and his cheating ways will escalate. Then eventually, he will get very careless with his cheating. Ladies, it's clear as day, if you do not meet his sexual needs, he will eventually cheat. It's important to adapt his Sexual Value system because it will help him not to cheat.

If a man is not sexually attracted to you because of your weight, he will keep another woman around until you lose weight, but in the meantime he will have sex with other women until he is fully attracted to you. Ladies, remember all men are not attracted to skinny women, so if you are a Big Woman, find a man who likes big women. When it comes to weight loss, women should pay attention to the signs a man gives her if he wants her to lose weight. For example, the man may make a small suggestion that explains how he wants a woman to wear certain clothes. When men cheat, it is different from when a woman cheats. Men are wired different from women because a man can have a fling and never catch feelings for the other woman. The other woman will just be a fill-in or a void for the man. With two women, a man can have a woman whom he loves and he can have the woman who he is physically attracted to. Men can have a main girl and a wife. The other woman will be his mistress. When a man has a mistress, he will not make her out to be his main woman because she is only there to fill a void in his relationship. Men get caught up when their cheating ways become more prevalent, and the other woman wants more. Over time, a fling that carries on for several months will become more than just a fling. The other woman would eventually demand more of his time, and for the cheating man, it will be difficult to keep the other woman secrete. This other woman will eventually want to take the place of a wife or the main woman. Ladies, remember, to catch a man cheating, you never have to look for him to cheat, in DUE TIME, HIS cheating ways will come to Light. You should never be naïve and overlook the signs of a cheating man because as he continues to cheat, he would eventually get lazy with his cheating ways. For example, if he tells you that he is always busy, or if he never spends holidays with you, or if he never let you meet any of his family members, or if he talks to you like he doesn't want you, and he calls you derogatory names, you might be the other woman.

CHAPTER 6—THE 80/20 RULE

(The Temptation guide for him and her)

As men, we need to pay attention to the 80/20 rule.
See we may be caught in-between two women,
and we find ourselves leaving our 80 percent for that 20 percent.
That 80 percent belongs to that woman who loves you, a good mother;
a true gift, that always uplift!!

She will be there to support in every way;
We don't realize it, until she no longer wants to stay!!
We see a woman that looks good;
*We chase it, acting like a fool, never paying attention to the **80/20 Rule.***

We leave our 80 percent, realizing that she was heaven sent.
Having a strong woman at home; but we leave her all alone.
But that 20 percent has a ravishing look, but she can't cook;
Always finding ways to tap into your black book!!

Your 80 percent might not have that ideal look,
but if you work with her, she will rewrite the book.
We disrespect her, leave her, because she gains a little weight,
but we should stick around and motivate;
stay around for her sake, and never leave her for something that's fake!
It's a shame; we leave our educated woman for a woman who can barely spell her name.

**Acting like a fool, never paying attention to the 80 / 20 Rule,
but unlike what Tyler Do,
I explain how the 80/20 Rule applies to you women too.**

*See you women will have a good man,
He doesn't have it all, but he stands tall, promising to never fall.
A good man that will put you first, he will try everything to quench your thirst.
See this 80 percent, is God sent, but you are too blind to see,
and you flee; all for that twenty!!*

*See this man continues to give, he even wrote your kids name in his will;
but you want a fake, money having thug,
you finally find out what he is all about; now you need a hug!!*

*Leaving your good man for someone who has more money;
not knowing that you are just another one on the list,
after he hit, you will get dismissed.
But you continue to chase all this 20 percent.
You may choose him because how you think he represent;*

*In the bedroom,
never paying attention to the **80/20 Rule** acting like a damn fool.*

*You think he puts in work,
deep down you know that he only wants your skirt,
but with that money, you love the way he flirt.
That real man, may not touch you, like you want him to,
But you need to teach him how to romance you.*

*Work with that man, and you both create a sexual plan.
But you wanted that 20, until that 20 raised up his hand.*

*But, you still choose, never paying attention to the **80/20 Rule**, acting like a fool.
You wanted the bad guy, not understanding why.*

Ladies and gentlemen, don't be a fooled, please choose the one who really loves you.

This is the 80/20 Rule

THE EXPLANATION = THE INTERPRETATION: THE 80_20 RULE

This poem really doesn't need any serious explanation. This poetic piece talks about temptation. When someone is in love, the Devil may send someone from the opposite sex to tempt a man or a woman. Before introducing this chapter, it's important to know that, men and women are tempted in different ways. Women temp men with sex, and men tempt women with money. Both men and women can be tempters when they are in a full committed relationship, and when someone is happy within their relationship, temptation always find a way to ease in.

His Temptation

Men are visual creatures and it is easy for us to get tempted by women. Ladies, it doesn't take much to tempt a man. When women wear certain clothes, they tempt us. When it comes to the opposite sex, men should practice techniques that block sexual gestures from woman who try to tempt us. One of these techniques could be to focus on your woman at home and think of how good she is to you. If a man is in a relationship, and he want his woman to commit, learning how to dealing with temptation is vital. Men, sometimes it's not always good to chase after a cute face and a sexy body. An outside woman with a sexy body and cute face may be more of a problem than a benefit. When you focus on a woman because of her looks, you may lose every time. You should never leave your "**FOR SHO for SOME MO.**" This statement simply means that: when you chase something that looks good, it is not always good, and in the process, you will lose your ideal woman. As men, we should recognize temptations and label it what is: (Temptation).

Macho Man Factor / the Victimized Man

Ladies, it may be difficult for a man to turn down sex because of the "**Macho Man Factor**." With the Macho Factor, the man is truly a victim. When women tempt men using the Macho Man Factor, the woman would seduce him and play on his sexuality. If he turns her down, she may try her best to test his manhood. Although he may be very secure with is sexuality, this woman targets his sexual preference because he turns her down. When this woman continues to pursue him and use the "Macho Man" factor, he may sleep with her to prove that he is a Macho Man!! She may play tricks on his mind and seduce him. Once he sleeps with her, she may think she has won him over, but in actuality, he does not have an emotional connection with her. When a man is a victim of the Macho Man Factor, he would simply have sex with the tempting woman, hoping, after the sexual encounter, she will leave him alone.

The Macho Man Factor is also used when the temptress tells the man: "You can do better than the one whom you are currently with." The temptress would glorify her sexual characteristics, and throw herself at him. This woman would repeatedly express how she is better than his current woman or his wife. She would tell him how his woman is not attractive, and she would also say things such as: "I can make love to you better than she can." When she says these things, this would usually cause him to sleep with her. Then, when he cheats, he might feel bad about the episode, but a mature, stable man would recognize when he is being placed in a sexual tempted trap. A mature man will always decline sexual offers made by a temptress. Men should realize that they can fall into a seductive woman's trap, and it's never ideal to leave an 80 percent woman for a 20 percent fling. Men, we should always be aware of the "female home wreaker."

Her Temptation

Like men, when it comes to relationships, women may think the grass is greener on the other side, but most of the times, the grass is not always greener. Ladies, when it comes to men, what looks like a winner, may not always be a winner. Women usually would find themselves being tempted by a man who has a lot of money and charisma, but this man may just want sex and not a committed relationship. After he sleeps with you, he would move on to the next woman. This tempting man tempts women by buying gifts and he would also provide romantic invitations. If you are a woman who falls for the tempting man, you may instantly lose the man whom is committed to you. When you cheat and fall for the tempting man, and if your boyfriend or your husband finds out, it will be very difficult for them to fully forgive you. When a woman cheats, it is harder for a man to forgive because the cheating woman targets the man's manhood and his pride. Ladies, when a woman cheats, men take it harder because there is nothing worse than knowing that another man was making love to your woman. When it comes to a woman being tempted by a man, women should always remember that, a man can be a wolf in sheep clothing. The tempting man is perceived to be a good man, but actually, this man might be controlling, rude, abusive and very arrogant. Women should recognize temptation, and it's important not to entertain temptation when it is introduced, especially if you are a woman who is in a happy relationship.

The Female Attraction

When a woman is very Jazzy, there would be several men who try to tempt her. If you are a woman who constantly has to fight temptation, its best to tell the tempting man that you are in a relationship and then, thank him for his advance, and cut the conversation short. Most women don't have a problem with doing this, but there are some women who fall victim to the tempting man. My womanizing friends tempted women all the time, and they have been very successful at getting women to sleep with them. When these men no longer wanted to deal with these women, they would brush them off like they were bad habits. If a woman has slight relationship problems, she becomes a prime target. Once the tempting man finds out that she has problems at home, he would attempt to romance her until she leaves her man.

Ladies, it's important to remember that all men who approach you while you are in a relationship are not always sent from the Devil. Remember, when a man approaches you, it doesn't mean that he want to bring harm to you. He might be there to take you away from your depressed and gloomy relationship. For example, although some of my womanizer friends may have had intentions to womanize a woman and only sleep with her, once they get to know that woman, they may have pursued a long-term, committed relationship with her. They would commit once they find out that they were equally yoked with that woman. They would also be very thankful that that woman decided to leave their man for them. When a womanizer approaches you, **You** may be the one who causes him to change his ways, and **He** may just be the one who takes you from your miserable, depressed relationship!! Sometimes, it may be fate to meet someone new. It's best to do a serious evaluation if you want to leave your present man for a new man. This concept is further explained in the "Answer" chapter.

CHAPTER 7—THE FRIEND ZONE

(Man's guide to get out of her "Friend Zone")

I am going to stop making you a priority while you make me an option!!!

With this Friend Zone, you constantly steal my time,
and you want me to spend my last dime,
and act as if you were mine.

I am tired of answering my phone, hoping that one day; I will get out of this Friend Zone.

I chase you because I want more, but you continue to tell me that, I am not what you are looking for;

You say things like: I am a good dude; you are not trying to be rude, but you always want me to take you out and pay for your food.

It's wrong, but I am in the Friend Zone, you constantly string me along.

You have several men to cater to your different needs.
You have that man, who will buy you everything,
he continues to bring, listening to the song you sing, not knowing he is tied to a string.

You have a man who you talk to, in hopes to be with you;
Then there's a Man who sexes you; you let him do everything to you;
Then, there's a Man who you want, but he don't want you.

So this is what I am going to do: **I am going to let you, do you!!**

You tell me about the men you use, you constantly tell me about the men you
choose, and you constantly want me to lose.

Sometimes it's my fault because in this Friend Zone, I get myself caught.
It's a Game and it's a Shame because deep down, you think that I am a Lame,
and with this Friend Zone, I even have a Name!!!

I am the cool dude who you talk to, the nice guy, who will never be able to make
love to you,
in times of troubles; I am the guy who you will run to,
when that other guy abuses you.
When, I am the real man; who wants to love you.

But Game *recognize* Game, I found me a woman; now things are not the same.
You stung me along; now;
you say I don't call, and now I'm wrong.

You are surprised of this lady that I have found, flipping your Friend Zone upside
Down;
With my new woman, I always score a Touchdown.

Like athletes dance in their end zone, I am dancing in your Friend Zone,
I have decided to leave you alone.

This is the Friend Zone!!

THE EXPLANATION = THE INTERPRETATION: FRIEND ZONE

This poetic piece explains the dreaded "Friend Zone." Although men
may place a woman in the Friend Zone, women are usually the ones
who place men in this zone. This chapter focuses on the characteristics
of a woman who places a man in her Friend Zone, and it also explains
how a man can overcome and benefit from her Friend Zone. When it
comes to a woman and her relationship with men, most women usually
have a man who serves a particular purpose in their life. These women
are not bad people, but they are opportunist. They prey on the weak

man, leaving him to ask, why doesn't she want to commit to me? These women have men who are sugar daddies. These women may have a man whom they will talk to on the telephone, knowing that they are not interested in him. These women would also have a man who gives them great sex, but they will never commit to this man because he usually doesn't have a job, and he is not husband material. The Friend Zone women may not tell her friends about this man because she want this man to stay secrete; for her, this man is only good for sex. When the Friend Zone woman has the sexual man in her life, she will never fully commit to him because she is embarrassed by him, but this man usually knows how to rock her world in the bedroom.

This woman may also have a man who she wants, but this man may not want her. If he gives her the opportunity, she would jump at the sound of his voice. She would plead and beg for his attention, but he would constantly turn her down; the more he turns her down, the least likely he will be trapped in her Friend Zone. While this man turns her down and treats her bad, she would continue to pursue him, but he would never want her because of how she treat and use other men. This woman has un-peculiar ways because she does not give the man who truly adores her, a chance, but she will keep him in the "Friend Zone." She will talk to this man, and flirt with him, but she will never sleep with him because she sees him as a nice guy or a lame that is not important.

Getting Out of her "Friend Zone"

Men, if we ever want to get out of the Friend Zone, you must first recognize that you are in the Friend Zone. When a woman calls you for sex, you benefit, but when she calls you to complain about another man, you lose every time. As men, we need to recognize that our ideal woman is waiting for us, and the Friend Zone is not a beneficial place for us. We should accept the fact that this Friend Zone woman is not interested in a relationship; we should move on and find us a woman who wants us. Men, if you continue to pursue this Friend Zone woman, you will continue to look like a lame. After several attempts, if this woman doesn't show interest, it's best to leave her alone and find a woman who shows interest in you.

To get out of the Friend Zone, you should reverse the Friend Zone and place her in the same Friend Zone. While dating this woman, you should talk about other women; you should talk about how other women pursue and desire you. Men, while dating the Friend Zone woman, it's important to let her know that she is just a Friend and she should pay for her meals when you all go out. When a man dates a woman who places him in the Friend Zone, that man should make sure he protects his cash!! Men, when you are in the Friend Zone, at all times, you must try your best to reap benefits of being this woman's friend. While on dates, you should ask her questions about how to sleep with other women. In her Friend Zone, it's also vital that you do not make yourself readily available. When you always make yourself readily available, it makes you appear to be weak or a lame. Time should be very limited with this Friend Zone woman, and when she starts to complain about time, you should tell her with a bold voice, "Well, you are not my woman, why should I give you all of my time? I have other women who I need to entertain." You should let the Friend Zone woman know that she is stopping your flow with other women, and she is not a priority in your life.

Although this woman may enjoy your company, you should make BOLD statements and let this woman know that she can't call you all the time because other women don't approve of her calls. Even if you don't have a girlfriend at the present moment, it's always best to act as if you do have a girlfriend. Once this happens, the Friend Zone woman will start to desire you because you perceive to have a woman. The Friend Zone woman will try her best to compete for your time. Eventually, this woman will get the point, and over time, she would stop playing games and leave you alone or become more than a friend. If she leaves you alone, it is very beneficial because now, you would have more time to pursue other women, and focus on improving your social well being. Once this woman decides to leave you alone, she will find another man and try to place him in the dreaded "Friend Zone."

Reverse & Benefit from the "Friend Zone"

Men, we can benefit from the Friend Zone. The first step you must take is: instantly place her into your Friend Zone. Don't try to sleep with this woman because she is to be looked at as if she is a sister or a friend who happens to be a female. With every conversation with this woman, you should either talk about women you currently date, or you should ask her to hook you up with her attractive friends. When you inquire about her friends, she would have difficulties perceiving you as a lame, and she would try to play match maker. Playing match maker benefits you because she may think she is doing a great dead by playing match maker with two friends; her male friend and her woman friend. For years, my womanizer friends slept with many women when they have applied this strategy!! They would accept the friend role and flip it for their benefit. When they had the chance, my womanizing friends would pursue the woman's friend. They would capitalize on the opportunity to date multiple friends of friends. Men, if you learn how to use the Friend Zone for your benefit, you would find yourself having multiple flings with multiple women.

To overcome the Friend Zone, you should attempt to make the Friend Zone woman unattractive in your eyes. You should search for this woman's flaws and her shortcomings. When you do this, you will not be overly attractive to her, and it will be easier to place her in your Friend Zone. When your attraction level for her decreases, you would learn how to give her less attention and time. Women love to be desired by men, and instantly, this Friend Zone woman will notice that you no longer give her all of your attention. Men, when you do this, you will make her out to be the lame; therefore making you the high commodity. As a man, it's important to understand that every woman has some type of flaw, and everyone, whether it's a male or female, we have some type of imperfections. At first, it might be difficult to find this woman's imperfections, but if you look hard enough, you will find them. Women usually go out of their way to make themselves look beautiful with make-up, fake nails, and fake hair. Making this woman unattractive would enable you to place her in your Friend Zone. For example, if she has average size breasts, you can use her average sized breast as a weapon against her, although you still want to have sex with her.

Men, if we have a homeboy, and he never pays for anything, and he always want you to pick up the tap, and he always want you to pick him up from his house, you would instantly think he was a FREE LOADER. So, why would you waste your time chasing a sexy, attractive woman whom you like, but she will never have sex with you or pursue a relationship? This woman always wants something from you; whether it's your time or your money, but you over look this because you think she is attractive. Why wouldn't you see this woman as a FREE LOADER? Men, with the Friend Zone woman, it doesn't make since for you to constantly take her out, talk to her all the time and NEVER reap any benefits. Why would you continue to let this woman use you? But, if your so called homeboy attempts to use you, you would instantly eliminate the friendship.

To fully reverse the woman's Friend Zone, you should recognize that you are in the Friend Zone. Then, you should maximize all the benefits of being her friend. Then, attempt to date all of her female friends. When you follow these strategies, you will love to be in the Friend Zone because you will start to date all of her friends, and most of the time her friends look better than they she does.

SECTION III

The Intimacy Chapters—*How to make her sexually commit*
The TOP TEN positions that guarantee's her orgasm

CHAPTER 8—LOVING YOU / ASKING WHY

(Guide to make her to sexually commit)

Massaging you with warm oil, relaxing you, I am ready to give you a clue that explains my love for you. Kissing and messaging your feet, it feels so good, you almost fall asleep; wonderful you are, making you glow like a midnight star. I love to be in your space; your love is full of grace. Sensation is what you bring; it's not a surprise that you have me attached to a string; you are an angel that makes the heavens sing.

Every man wants to be close to you, but he has to be **One Hundred Percent** because you are so **Self-Sufficient**. You hold the gates of sex; a man can't enter unless you give him permission to make your body flex. You deserve a man who will go down to prove his love, with you being so *wet*; understanding what you *hold*, making me *strong* and *bold*, being with you is like having the earth's richest *gold*. The creator give you *that* precious gift, which is so magnificent, being with you is pure excitement. A woman that is so sexy, and so rich with beauty, *you have no clue*, how Loving you—would be so nice to do . . .

Loving You

Why?

Why, asking why, as I look into your eyes. A woman that is so neat, filled with class, but also sweet. Once you walk the Earth you send a Silent Alarm because you are built in the most Perfect Form. With the question, Why, your looks, your moves and especially your clues? With your skin, oh' so smooth, romancing is the only way to loom to you. The things you'll make a man want to do. Nubian queen, you fulfill every man's dream, goddess of Love, asking why do you hold the power of love? Maybe you are an angel that comes from the heavens? With light shining on you, you are a fantasy that is oh' so true. Asking why, your presence makes me feel alive; your beauty makes me strive

Asking Why?

THE EXPLANATION = THE INTERPRETATION: LOVING YOU AND ASKING WHY

A pastor once stated: God gave us sex as a gift, and sex is not intended to be bad, because God provided us with our sexuality. Sex is one of God's most precious gifts; sex was also meant to be more than procreative; it was also intended be pleasurable. The Loving You and Asking Why chapter explains how a man can sleep with a woman on the first date upon entering his home. This chapter also explains the importance of pleasing a woman and making her feel relaxed. This chapter also explains how to soothe a woman's body with a relaxed atmosphere. As men, we should understand that women or unique and they are very different from us, and when we make love to a woman's mind, making love to her body comes easy. If a woman is intrigued by you, whether she likes your swag, your touch or the way you talk; when you make love to her mind, she will not hold back during sex. She will be prone to have multiple orgasms.

To get a woman to sexually commit, first you should make her feel sexy. Once she feels sexy, she will be comfortable around you, and she will give herself to you. Men, if you want to sleep with a woman, whether you sleep with her on the first night, or after a couple of dates, or if we do the right thing and marry her before sex, you should always make her feel comfortable and sexy before the intimacy. **Women are like chicken: after you bake or boil it, once it is done, the meat fall right off the bones.** Once a woman is warm and hot, she gets in the mood, and she will be ready to make love. Men, we make mistakes when we fail to get a woman in the mood before sex. We are different from women because we can easily get an erection, and we don't have to be in the mood if a woman is very attractive, but a woman must be relaxed, massaged, and romanced before she will let you make love to her.

One Night Stand and the "Pad Swagger"

Although the one night stand is considered morally incorrect, it does happen. It's a secret to get a woman to give it up on the first night. We sometimes can get overly anxious when it comes to sexing a woman. We may desperately want to have sex with her, but if we stay patient and the mood is right, she will fall right in your arms. First, you should never talk about sex before inviting a woman up to your home for a night cap. If you talk about sex, she will think that you had a motive to sleep with her, and she will be on the defensive side the entire night. We should never give a strong sexual motive because a woman never wants to come off as easy or promiscuous, although there is the occasional woman who loves one night stands!! It's always important to know, women want to have sex as much as men, but after a one night stand, they will make the sexual encounter feel like an accident, although they wanted to have sex as much as we did. When a one night stands occur, it's always important to express that things just lead to one thing after the other. It's also important to explain that you don't look at her differently because she sexually committed on the first date.

It's a proven strategy that can be used to get a woman to sleep with you, whether it's on the first date or if it's after a couple of dates. First, you must make sure that your home is the true bachelor pad. Your place of resident should make her feel like she has stepped into something that is intriguing. Your home should be neatly cleaned with a nice aroma. You should treat your home with the same swagger that you posses as a man. When your home is very comfortable, it will make the woman want to instantly take off her clothes. If possible, you should try to invest in the latest electronics such as flat screen televisions and a nice laptop or a nice desktop computer. Men, it would also be nice if you display your intellectual side. You can have a bookcase that contains intriguing books of some sort. Everyone is unique, so, each pad should have its uniqueness. Your home should have a "Pad Swagger." It's best to choose the ideal "**Pad Swagger**" that makes your home very unique and cozy. When this is accomplished, when a woman enters your home, she will love the uniqueness of the home, and she will want to take off her clothes. When the home is clean with the right pad swag, she would become very comfortable, especially if she has a couple of drinks or some type of drug that makes her intoxicated. A clean and cozy home will always entice a woman into taking off her clothes. As men, we should offer her something to drink, and if she accepts your offer, you should give her something to drink in a clean glass. You should never offer a woman something to drink from a paper cup or a coffee mug, unless she requests otherwise.

Offering a woman something to drink out of a clean glass will make her feel very comfortable. After drinks are served, it's important to ask her if she would like to watch a movie, and while the movie is playing, you should make sure the lights are dim; while the movie is playing and the lights are dim, she will continue to relax herself making it easier and easier for you to ease off her panties. As men, we should understand that watching a movie is not the only way to get a woman to ease off her panties. There are several other ways to entice her into sleeping with us. A woman must be in a clean, comfortable, intriguing environment, and after being in such an environment, she will be warm enough to sexually treat you. If she thinks you are attractive, and she digs your pad swagger, you will be surprised how easily it will be for you to get her goodies. Although watching a movie is ideal, it doesn't matter if you decide to watch a movie, as long as your pad makes her very relaxed. For example, you can give her a back or foot massage, eat an elegant dinner, or listen to a variety of music to get her in the mood. In a comfortable, clean and intriguing environment, she will be ready to sexually commit. Remember, once she decides to sexually commit, you we must represent in the bedroom. To represent in the bedroom, you should visit chapter 10, the *TOP TEN sex positions that guarantee's her orgasm.*

CHAPTER 9—BEING INTIMATE

(Guide to keep her sexually satisfied)

Deep Stroke, after deep stroke, making you so wet;
You feel like a warm **Shower**, letting your pussy feel my **Immaculate Power**;
Long deep stokes, after long deep stroke;

Making you grip my shoulders while you caress my **head**, with your legs **spread**,
You hold my body and you explode on my luxurious **bed**.

As I repeatedly taste your inner **thighs**, you beg me to come **inside**.
With your bosom ready to **ignite**, tasting you is such a **delight**,
You moan because the feeling is out of **sight**.

Turning you over, spreading your hips;
Sliding my fingers between you,
Before giving you this love clue, again and again, I taste you.

Your pussy screams **Excitement**; your lips experience a true **Enlightenment**.

I pounce on you with such a **thrust**; this is more than **just, Lust**.
I love you so **much** because of this intimate **touch**.

I am a Lion, and you are my **Lioness**.
So deep,
You feel every inch of **this**,
The feeling is oh'so **intense**.

One hundred and one ways, I find ways to pleasure it, the long stroke, I have
Mastered it,
This is how you make me **Represent**.
You will always think of it!!

This is me
Being Intimate

THE EXPLANATION = THE INTERPRETATION: BEING INTIMATE

This poetic piece introduces the "Being Intimate" guide. This chapter speaks directly to men, but women will find this section very interesting because it explains the techniques he must apply in the bedroom if you want to experience the ultimate orgasm. Men, when it comes to sexing a woman, you must understand the techniques of getting her aroused. If she experiences an out of sight sexual experience, she will sexually commit and stay committed. There are secretes to make a woman moan, scream, and explode with the ultimate orgasm. After reading and studying this chapter, you would understand how to instantly sexually satisfy a woman. This chapter also explains how you should make her feel desirable when sexing her. Upon sexing her, you should have a dominate attitude that reaps confidence. When you have confidence in the bedroom, she will have an outstanding sexual experience. In the bedroom, you should always have the attitude of an **ALPHA MALE.**

Men, before sexing her, it's important that *you do not* express how you will pound her pussy, which is better known as her Sweet Spot. Before sexing her, you should simply let her experience the sexual encounter for herself. It is recommended that you surprise her with a pleasant pussy pounding. While sexing her, you should learn how to control your sexual emotions. Controlling your sexual emotions would help you keep a longer erection. As her pussy gets wet, it's best to stay focus while in her. Doing sex, you should think about dominating her sweet spot!! This is very important because if you excessively enjoy and meditate on how good it feels while stroking her sweet spot; you would have a quick ejaculation. Let her enjoy the Dick strokes, but when you want to ejaculate, simply think about how awesome the pussy is, and then explode in her.

Men, we should understand that we should dominate her pussy. Upon the first time having sex with a woman, if your sex is horrible, she may never speak to you again; so it is important to sex her with a lot of passion and dominance. If you don't feel up to having sex with her, turn her down because if you have bad sex, she may regret sleeping with you, and you may never get a second chance to sex her. As a matter of fact, if you turn her down, it may turn her on, and when the time is right, you should sex her right.

Every woman is different and after horrible sex, she may give you a second chance to prove your dominance, but this is not always the case. If she gives you a second chance to prove yourself, it's vital that you sex her sweet spot the right way. You may have to perform an intimate kiss on her sweet spot or you may have to simply pound it until she screams your name. When sexing her sweet spot, sometimes, we cannot help ourselves with a swift ejaculation, especially if her sweet spot is very wet and tight. If a swift ejaculation occurs, you must tell her that it was the sweetest, wettest that you have ever had. Make sure that she understands why you came very quickly. After your first ejaculation, you must not be afraid to lick her or suck on her breast until you can obtain another erection. You must keep her aroused at all times; sucking and licking her sweet spot is a great way to keep her turned on. Upon dating several lesbian women, I have learned how these women please each other with the sensation of the tongue, and it is very important that you learn the "Wet Mouth," technique that will be fully explained in the next chapter of this book. A true combination of the "Wet Mouth," as well as a good DICK pounding will have a woman Dick Whipped, causing her to commit.

If a woman is clean, and she smells fresh, you should never be afraid to lick on her sweet spot. Licking and sucking on her sweet spot may sound odd, but a woman's sweet spot is a very intimate place on her body. So, as men we should never be afraid to perform an intimate kiss on her. When licking her sweet spot, you should first start with her clitoris, and then place your entire mouth over her until she moans and releases her juices into your mouth. **Note:** when licking and sucking on her sweet spot, you should never be rough, but you should kiss her with swift, fast or slow passionate licks with the tongue. When she has an orgasm, you don't have to swallow her juices; you can simply let her juices flow over our tongue onto the bed, etc.

Licking her sweet spot may not be your first choice upon an initial ejaculation; but it's your call. You can suggest that she slightly rub your balls and your penis until you get another erection. Upon rubbing of the balls, you should ask her with a slight authority to kiss your penis. Once she kisses your penis, she is very likely to finish the job by gracefully sucking it until your erection comes back. Once the erection occurs, you MUST sex her passionately with long deep strokes until she calls you the Big "D" Bandit.

Men, we should never waste a hard erection, and we should always remember that a woman's sweet spot is made to be pounded. It's fine to make love to her, but she always desires a good pussy pounding. Doing sex, women want to be handled, and they will let you know if they want to be sexed fast or slow. Doing sex, it's best to talk dirty to her, then be quite and continue to pound her sweet spot. Although pounding her sweet spot is ideal, you should make sure that you mix up the pounding with slow intimate deep strokes.

When you sex her on a regular basis, you need to have a mixture. While sexing her, you should thoroughly touch her with aggressive long deep stroking motions. With aggressive deep strokes, she will fall in love with every intimate moment. Equally, a woman desires to be a slut in the bedroom, but she also desires to be a lady. So, sexing her passionately with long deep strokes and making her moan and scream will keep her Dick Whipped. After receiving some good Dick, most women want to be hugged and caressed, but if you are exhausted, tell her to give you a minute to get yourself together. Let her know that you need to let your muscles relax for a second. Men, when you hold her after great sex, she would love to be in your arms. She will love the romantic experience. She would open up her mind and once her mind is fully opened, it will be very easy to make her have an orgasm every time you have sex with her.

Becoming the Big "D" Bandit

A woman wants a man to put it on her!! I repeat, a woman wants a man to put it on her!! If she is a big girl, a thick girl or a small girl, women must feel the Dick!! Doing sex, if you pound her sweet spot, and keep stroking her until she scratches on your back, she will be very thankful to have the DICK pounding experience. While sexing her, you should pound her sweet spot because women love when men reach their G Spot. The "G" Spot is a spot at the bottom of the woman's pussy and it drives them crazy when it is repeatedly pounded.

When you pound her sweet spot, and go deeper inside of her, she will view you as the "**Big Dick Bandit**." You should know your limitations when it comes to your size; so, if your woman thinks that you have a small manhood, it's important to offset your small penis. With a small penis, you are at a disadvantage when it comes to pounding her pussy, but don't be worry. With a small manhood, you must learn how to lick, suck and touch her. This would help her reach multiple orgasms. It's important to understand, a woman has 100 and 1 ways to be turned on, and it is your job to try to touch all of her spots. Remember, you can kiss her neck, squeeze her ass while fucking her, suck on her breast and slightly pull her hair all at the same time while telling her how sweet and wet her pussy is. Later in this book, there are ten sexual positions that are recommended for the bedroom, and these positions should be used if you want her to sexually commit and stay committed.

Getting her "D" whipped

When you sex a woman the right way, there is a great possibility that she will become "**Dick Whipped**." When a she is "Dick Whipped," she will have sex with you anywhere. Your goal is to keep her coming back for more. If she is "Dick Whipped," she will be crazy for your love, and she will be less likely to cheat. She will let you drive her car, she will buy you clothes and she will think about you sexing her sweet spot while she is at work or when she is relaxing at home. When a woman is "Dick Whipped," she will not only want to make love to you, but she will want to suck on you every time she sees you. Once a man becomes the Big Dick Bandit and he has her Dick Whipped, his Dick will become the woman's best friend; **NOTE:** like the woman private parts, your private parts must stay clean and fresh if you want her to suck on you.

CHAPTER 10—THE ART OF PASSION

(Guide to the TOP TEN sex positions that guarantee's her orgasm)

    *The art of passion is something shared when I'm in your presence. Looking at you is a dream that comes true. You are like the sweetest rose, wanting to kiss you from your head to your toes, showering you with love that is ever so bold. By your side is a place where every man wants to be, but that place is only reserved for me; Asking could I spoil you with millions of treats? You make the strongest knight want to sweep you off of your feet. You are the Princess of Love. There is no other way to explain thee, someone with such **beauty**; your kind comes once every **century**. Wanting to kiss you there, you ask where, quickly responding everywhere, licking on your cl*tor*s making you swear, you would make me answer to the most strongest dare.*

    Your sexual sensation is forever lasting, that's why being with you is the Art of Passion

THE EXPLANATION = THE INTERPRETATION: THE ART OF PASSION

Sex the Art of Love Making

Sex is very important while attempting to make a woman fully commit, and there is an Art to Love Making. This section explains multiple sexual positions that will keep her coming back. These are the Top 10 most desirable sex positions that guarantee's her orgasm. If you sex her correctly the first time, she will be sprung off your love. To get a woman to become "**Dick Whipped**," and have her call you the "**Big Dick Bandit**," it's important to incorporate the following sexual positions into your bedroom. Although it might take practice to fully master these positions, once all 10 positions have been mastered, she will always become your sexual treat.

The Top Ten Sex Positions (Make her Commit)

(1.) First, there is the "**Backwards and Forward Vertical Pleasure**." This position is when the man is on top of the woman and she closes her legs and he strokes her deeply. The Backward Vertical Pleasure is ideal because the woman is face down with her backside upward. With this position, the man penetrates her as if it was a doggy style position, but she will lay with her legs closed. **Warning**: With this position, the man has to have at least a six inch penis. If he lack at least six inches, he will not be able to fully penetrate the woman causing great frustration in the bedroom, especially if the she has a large back side.

(2.) Then, there is the "**Sexual Rodeo**." This is a classic position. The woman is on top of the man, and she rides him like he is a bull. The Sexual Rodeo can be done backwards or forward depending on the couple's desires. To cause a deeper penetration, the man can have the woman lay down on him while her legs are bent, and he can then hold and squeeze her ass tightly, and then he should take control by swiftly stroking her passionately. She will start to moan and she will enjoy the swift pounding of her sweet spot.

(3.) Then, there is the "**Galaxy**." With the Galaxy, the man should lay next to the woman. While laying next to her, he strokes her from the side. For the woman, one leg should lie across him in a bent formation while he penetrates her from the side. While penetrating her, he should constantly play with her clitoris causing an arousing sensation.

(4.) Then, there is the "**Bunge Thrust**." With the Bunge Thrust, the man faces the woman, and places her legs over his shoulders. He then strokes her very intimately. With the Bunge Thrust, she leans her head off the side of the bed causing her to have a head rush. The man should penetrate her deeply with a lot of passion and excitement.

(5.) Then, there is the "**Triple Threat**." With the Triple Threat, the man lay on top of the woman, and while stroking her, he lean to the woman's left side and suck on her left breast. While leaning to her left, he sucks on her left breast, then, he takes his left or right hand and gently plays with her clitoris, causing a great sensation. With the Triple Threat position, the man strokes the woman with is DICK, plays with the woman's clitoris and suck on her breast all at the same time, giving her the **Triple Threat!!!** If he can sustain this pleasure for five to ten minutes, she will have an ultimate orgasm.

(6.) Then there is, his and her: "**Taste**" and "**Wet Mouth**" positions. This position was explained in earlier, but in this section, it is explained in greater details. With the Taste and the Wet Mouth position for her, the woman lays flat on her back, and the man let his tongue and mouth do all the work. The man would let his tongue slide up and down the woman's sweet spot and he must repeatedly kiss her. He should repeatedly suck on her clitoris causing a true love experience for her. He should become very familiar with her sweet spot by constantly slurping and sucking on it letting her juices flow over his tongue and throughout his teeth. With this position, he should also hums on her clitoris. He can also place ice in his mouth while repeatedly tongue kissing her. He can also perform the Taste/Wet Mouth position while the woman is on her knees. With this position, he should have her in a doggy style position, and he should lie on his back. While lying on his back, he should gracefully pull himself closely to her and slurp and kiss her. He should passionately slurp on her, passionately kissing her, and let her juices run down his face. The kissing and slurping should be done until she is completely satisfied.

Her Wet Mouth

The man should also entice the woman to perform the *Taste/Wet Mouth position*. Once a woman is very familiar with the man's manhood, she can ask him, "how does he like it? slow, fast or a mixture of the two." To successfully perform the woman's Wet Mouth; the woman should suck on him like his manhood is her best friend. She can either perform her Taste or the Wet Mouth position by lying down next to him or she can have him lay on the bed while his penis is erect. She can also have him stand up while she performs her wet mouth position. When the man is in a standing position, she should be on her knees. While she is on her knees, she can repeatedly suck on him fast or slow, but the succulent motion should be very passionate. It is also recommended that she place her hands on the balls, and she should massage the balls very gently. When a woman sucks on him, she will feel herself getting very turned on by his sexual body movements and his sexual moan and groans. The woman's pussy should become very wet and juicy, and she will want to feel his hard erection inside her.

With the Taste/Wet Mouth position, the woman should also perform different succulent methods on the balls. Not only should she suck his manhood, she should gently place his balls in her mouth and hum on the balls. This succulent method should make him groan and want more and more of her wet mouth. Women should remember that the balls are very gentle and while sucking the balls, they should also be licked. With her Wet Mouth/Taste position, the woman can also lick the portion right under the man's balls. This part of the man's body is called the Gush area, and it is unlike any other area on his body. If the woman's wet mouth is done correctly, the man will commit. She will be considered a keeper!!!!

The Wet Mouth/Taste position also introduces the **Peach Pie and Ice Cream Technique.** With this technique, the woman should place Peach Pie and Ice Cream on a plate or in a small bowl. Then she should feed him both pie and the ice cream, and while the pie and ice cream melts in his mouth, the woman should gently massage the man's penis and balls and perform oral sex on him. The woman should perform her sexual acts until the ice cream and pie fully melts in his mouth. Then after the pie and ice cream has fully melted in his mouth, she should feed him another spoon until all of the ice cream and peach pie is completely gone. With this technique, only the man should have ice cream and pie in his mouth. He will taste the sweet pie and the sweet ice cream while experiencing an intimate massage on his manhood. His taste buds will explode, and his penis will experience an ultimate arousal. Remember, only the man should have the ice cream and pie in his mouth, and between pleasing him, the woman should feed him with another scoop of ice cream and pie until the pie and ice cream is completely gone. This can be a very inexpensive technique because the Peach Pie should be a small microwaveable pie which can be purchased at your local shopping market.

(7.) Then, there is: the "**Hitting it Thug Style**," the Dogging it Out position. With this position, the woman's backside is facing the man. The man penetrates the woman's pussy/her sweet spot and he constantly stroke her repeatedly with long deep strokes. With this position, the man should be in control by penetrating her. He should have a thug mentality while stroking her, and he should stoke her with a lot of passion. The deep strokes should be applied to the woman deeply and passionately. He should stroke her as if he has been incarcerated or in prison for three to five months. With this style, her pussy is pounded from the back, and the man should slightly pull her hair while administering the pounding. **NOTE**: pulling of the hair should be gracefully done, and it's important not to overdo it. The roughness should be done with the Dick, and not by choking the woman or pulling out her hair.

(8.) Then, there is the "**Baby Boy.**" With the Baby Boy position, the man picks the woman up in a standing position, and the woman holds on to him tightly. While the man stands, the woman lets him penetrate her. She would have her arms and legs wrapped around him while she is completely off the ground. The man hops around the bedroom constantly thrusting her pussy. This position was first introduced in the movie, "Baby Boy." With the Baby Boy position, the man can show his dominance and his strength while pounding her sweet spot. If the man cannot pick up the woman, its best to perform the "**Baby Boy-Sensation**" position. With this position, the woman faces the wall, and the man stands behind her, and he strokes her from the back causing her to be pinned against the wall. With this position, he also shows off his dominance by stroking her and pinning her to the wall. The man can also perform the "**Baby Boy-Freak Nasty.**" The "Baby Boy-Freak Nasty" position is when the man stands behind the woman, and the woman touches her toes while he passionately strokes her pussy from behind. With this position, the woman experience a head rush because she touches her toes in a standing position. While standing, she will receive the ultimate Dick penetration, making her stay sexually committed.

(9.)   Then there is the "**Being Intimate**" position. This position is recommended for couples who are very much into each other. With this position, the man is on top of the woman. The man constantly penetrates the woman while she rubs his back. With this position, the man and the woman whispers softly in each other's ears and tell each other how much they love one another. Both, the man and the woman whisper to each other all the things that they love about each other. With this position, there is a lot of talking involved. Several complements are given and intimacy is fully achieved. **WARNING:** due to the mass amount of talking involved with this position, both the man and the woman should make sure that they do not call out an ex-lover's name!!!!

(10.) Then there is "**Jungle Love.**" With Jungle Love, the couple's freestyle all of the positions listed above until both, the man and the woman are exhausted and they fall asleep naked!!!

SECTION IV

Love and Marriage—*Making her a Keepsake*

*Houses and wealth are inherited from parents, but a prudent
wife is from the LORD.*

Proverbs 19:14 (NIV)

Chapter 11—TIME

(Man's guide to making her a keepsake)

Can I give you my time? There are 24 hours in a day. I want to romance you in every way. Your sweet sensation-eases my day. The time spent with you is a dream come true. Dropping down to one knee to explain the "T." The "T" means that we are always be together, you are as soft as a feather, and your beauty is ever so clever. The "I" is for intensity: For me, you are the one and only. When time is spent, there is evidence that you are heaven sent. The "M" is for every moment that I am with you. For every moment that you are in my life, I will make the strongest sacrifice. Finally, there is the "E," which stands for everlasting—Your love is so everlasting. It is hard to explain what sensation you bring. When I am with you, I feel wonderful things. That's why, time spent with you is such a magnificent thing.

-Time

The Explanation = The Interpretation: TIME

This section starts with the element of **TIME**. Women fall in love with this poetic piece because it talks about something that woman deeply care about, and that's **TIME**. When a man and a woman are in a relationship, it's important that both, the man and the woman understand the importance of balancing their careers, family, and friends. If a man or a woman does not have **TIME** for one another, it would be difficult for their relationship to survive. If **TIME** is *not* spent, one person in the relationship will start to feel a void, or they may feel neglected. To build a relationship, and sustain a healthy relationship, it takes **TIME**. Sometimes a man or a woman should know how to enjoy their own company, but it's very importance to spend **TIME** with their mate.

When it comes to **TIME**, communication and being honest is very important. Men and women must be honest with themselves before they decide to get into a committed relationship. Being in a relationship requires work, therefore, it requires **TIME**. Both, men and women should be aware that there are 24 hours in a day, and every hour should be accounted for because once the day is gone, that day no longer exist. Due to the fact that every day is a special day, both the man's time and the woman's time should be appreciated.

Sometimes a man or a woman's job may be very demanding, and due to these demands, it may be difficult to work around one's schedule. If this is so, the man or the woman should communicate with one another and explain the demands of their jobs. For example, if a man works two jobs; **TIME** should still be set aside for that woman. If he has a job that requires him to travel, his mate should understand that he may be out of town for long periods. If he works a lot, he should show his appreciation when he comes home by spending **TIME** with his woman. For example, when the 44th president of the United States, Barack Obama, ran for president, his wife Michelle Obama had to wait for him while he was out on the campaign trail. His job required him to be away from home. It was clear and concise, that as a couple, they had a wonderful communication channel when it came to allocating their **TIME**. Understanding that the future president had a job to do while he was on the campaign trail, the future First Lady never perceived Barack Obama to be a cheater. While running for president, the media never reported any infidelity issues amongst the couple. While on the campaign trail, Barack was gone for weeks at a time and we never heard of him cheating or sleeping with other women. Candidate Barack Obama and future First Lady of the United States of America never had any noticeable issues about their **TIME** spent with each other. Michelle Obama understood that Barack had a job to do, and it was all worth it because he became the 44th president of the United States. Women shouldn't complain or nag when their man is out doing his job. If a woman supports her man, her man would show a great appreciation towards her when **TIME** allows him to. Women are not the only ones that should know the importance of **TIME**; men should also understand that **TIME** can be a major constraint on a relationship, causing a woman not to commit.

Ladies, while you are in a relationship, and your man is at work, you should never let external forces convince you that your man is out cheating. Women usually let their friends pursued them to think that their man is out cheating when he is out making an honest living. If you suspect that your man is cheating, you should not make assumptions about cheating. If you think he is spending his **TIME** with someone else, you should go directly to the source and ask him about cheating. If he is cheating, and he is spending his **TIME** with someone else, it will be brought to the surface, and his cheating ways will be exposed. False cheating allegations may be distractions for not only the man, but for the woman as well.

When it comes to **TIME** and being in a healthy relationship, men and women must trust each other. Although a man or a woman may work long hours, it doesn't mean that they are out cheating or doing something that they do not have any business doing. Men and women should always give each other the benefit of the doubt when it comes to having a monogamous relationship. When couples share each other's **TIME**, there should be a clear and concise agreement between the man and the woman. For example, if a man or a woman has other obligations, it is best to communicate the **TIME** constraints. No matter how bad each party wants to be in a relationship, it's important to be honest about **TIME** constraints. Being honest will help eliminate unwanted problems within the relationship. If there are **TIME** constraints, and one member of the relationship does not have the time, the other party might feel pressured to be in that relationship. The pressure to commit may cause great frustration for someone who doesn't have time. If a man or woman keeps complaining about **TIME** not being allocated, a conversation should be held between the man and the woman. Both parties should decide how they can or cannot spend more time together. If either, the woman or the man requires more time, but time cannot be allocated, the woman or the man might have to go their separate ways until a compromise has been met.

If a woman supports her man after he has placed her under great **TIME** constraints, he should reward her for her sacrifices. He should treat her with gifts because of her sacrifices. When he acknowledges her **TIME** sacrifices, she will fully commit to him. Although, this chapter leans towards men making **TIME** for women, women should also make time for their man. **TIME** spent should be a wonderful experience for couples, and when the necessary sacrifices are made, both the man and the woman should indulge in each other's love. It's always important to remember that: men and women will make **TIME** for what they want to make **TIME** for, and if they want to be in a relationship, they will make **TIME** sacrifices.

CHAPTER 12—THE HOLIDAYS

(Man's guide to making her a keepsake)

Valentine's Day

Today is not just another day, it's Valentine's Day.
It's a day that is easy to *Evaluate*,
360 degrees, your love continues to *Rotate*,
In you, I find ways to *Elevate*, because you continue to *Motivate*.
Explaining how you are an *Inspiration*,
You are an unforgettable *Celebration*;
With instant *Gratification*; we can create several strong *Generations*,
It's clear that you are one of God's most elegant *Creations*.
You are an Angel; I will not be *Naive*, and *Believe* that
As this day comes to an *Ease*,
Your beautiful intuition will ever *Leave*.
You are my tremendous start; explaining,
How you will forever hold my heart.
You are the ***epitome'*** of this day,
This is why I have to say;

Happy,
Valentine's
Day

THE EXPLANATION = THE INTERPRETATION: THE HOLIDAYS

This poetic piece was created for the day of love, Valentine's Day. It opens the discussion of the importance of spending time with your mate on special days such as anniversaries, family reunions, birthdays and holidays, etc. If a man wants to be with a woman, it's recommended that he spend holidays with her. For some strange reason, women love holidays and special events. For example, a woman will remember her first kiss, her first date, or her first time she met the man of her dreams. Men, if we want our woman to commit, it's important to acknowledge her on special days, whether it's her birthday, Valentine's Day or Christmas. It's also important to remember anniversaries, and holidays such as Thanksgiving and Memorial Day. To get a woman to commit and stay committed, it is also important to invite her to the occasional family reunion. It's always good to show her that, one day, she may have the opportunity to be part of your family. Men, even if she declines your offer to attend one of these special days, it's always the thought that counts. When a woman receives such invites, they feel very special. If you are really into a woman, it's always a great idea to share the holidays with her, and if she is really into you, she will be more than happy to spend this time with you.

Holidays are special days set aside by God, and couples should experience them together. When holidays are spent together, couples experience a very intimate time with each other. A woman is a gift, and on special days, such as Valentine's Day, you should make sure she feels appreciated. On birthdays and on Mother's Day, it's always a great idea to send her flowers, candy or a fruit basket to her job. When men send flowers to a woman's job, she would become the envy amongst her female co-workers. Upon receiving flowers or any other special acknowledgement, she will never forget the acknowledgement. On that day, she will brag to her co-workers how wonderful she thinks you are. Sending gifts to her job will always give you commitment points. Again, men, on special days, a woman must be cherished if you want her to commit.

Chapter 13—Your Romance

(Man's guide to making her a keepsake)

What does your romance really mean?
Maybe it's a fictional *thing*, but when I am with you,
You make my soul *Sing*; your presence heightens my **Day**,
This *sensation* makes me **Stay**.

With your **Taste** being so **Sweet**,
Looking at you reminds me that you are an unforgettable **Treat**.
Taking you on a romantic cruise, as we sleep amongst the **Seas**,
Your love puts me at **Ease**.

You make me feel like a king; as I kiss a rose and lay you **Down**,
Your romance helps me wear this unseen **Crown**.
What does your romance really mean?
Is it a fictional *thing*? Maybe not, because this sensitivity is **oh'so Real**,
Your romance has my heart **Sealed**.

As we take trips to other countries; this would be so **elegant**,
because your romance is very **extravagant**.
This is something that you give;
Your romance provides a . . . . breathtaking **Thrill**.

Your Romance . . . from my lips, to your heart . . . Explaining your Romance

THE EXPLANATION = THE INTERPRETATION: YOUR ROMANCE

When dating, men and woman should understand how Romance plays a major role in a relationship. This poetic piece was written for the woman, and it is designed for a man to give this poetic piece to her. The poetic peice explains her Romance. It touches on how great it is to experiece her Romance. Being romatic goes far beyong having sex with a woman. When it comes to making a woman commit or stay commited, it's imporatant to go on dates with her. If money is tight, you should spend time with her by doing recreational things that do not require a lot money. You and your woman can take long walks in the park; you can go to museams, or you and her can rent a $1.20 movie and snuggle up with one another. Being romantic can be explained when couples get to know each other's most intimate thoughts and their most deepest feelings. Although, men and women can experience unconditional love, love is something that is created once two people get to know one another.

Love should not be taken for granted. When someone is in love, that person may think about the other person night and day. When someone falls in love, they are usally in love with their uniquenes, and everyone is unique in their own special way. Love is usually built around a person's charactirstics and their sense of homour. Whether, it's a person's charisma, a person's swag or a person's conversations, love is usually created through Romance. To stay in love, couples need to be practice being romantic with eachother. Being romantic also creates memories. A romantic experience may occur when a man and a woman attend a theatrical play, attend a concert or when they intimately learn eachother. A romantic experience is also created when couples go to church and worship together. Throughout a relationship, it does not matter how long the couple has been together, whether its 2 months, 2 years or 20 years, couples should continue to Romance each other. Although dating can be very expensive at times, it's important to have several romantic episodes, expecially when you are trying to make someone commit. Being romantic is the essence of being in love, and after an romantic episode, love making is very intense.

While experiencing a romantic experience, couples should learn their mate's most intimate desires, needs and wants. With a romantic experience, couples should also learn their mates future plans as well as their upbringing. A romantic experience can also occur when two couples spend hours talking to eachother on the phone. As this poetic piece expresses: "is your romance a fictional thing," this simply explains that the romantic experience is so out of sight and the man is high off of her mind and soul. In this poetic piece, he also charishes the moment of being in the woman's presence.

A romantic experience can also occur when the man or the woman massages eachother's back, feet or hands. The romantic experience can also be when a man sparingly calls a woman at work and tell her that she is special. This type of experience can also occur when a man randomly sends his woman flowers to her job. The more romantic experiences couples have, the more that couple will commit and stay committed to one another.

Again, dating is essential to a relationship, and a romantic experience can also be reached when a woman experiences a sporting event with her man; this would usually be something that a man likes to do. Men love sports, and when women take time to learn and experience sports with their man, he would be more likely to visit a theatrical play or a romantic love comedy. Most of the time, when couples have a "Free Romantic Experience," its better than having a very expensive "Romantic Experience" because a "Free Romantic Experience" usually is very personal for the couple. When a man or a woman continues to experience romantic experiences, they would know what makes a person happy or sad. Having several romantic experinces help improve love and the overal health of the relationship, making the couple commit and stay commited.

CHAPTER 14—CORPORATE MERGER

(Couples guide: The identity of Marriage-the commitment)

This Corporate Merger;
Two businesses entities coming together to create **One** strong **Institution**.
My currency and your products, it's all about securities and trust.
Oh' how they will love us: one of a kind, as we celebrate over the finest wine.

The two of us, coming together to create great wealth,
being customers of each other's love; we find ways to **strive**,
as our stock **rise**, we keep this relationship **alive**.

Our competition tries to infiltrate and find ways to tax our love,
but we continue to have a sexual gain, our cost analysis will never change.
We have one heartbeat, which creates a personal monopoly.
With our **revenue**, we have maximized our business **value**.

Our corporate merger has created a superb business relationship with an astonishing
sexual relationship, with an extravagant, business intent: **All in this Competitive
Environment.**
We are the envy of our rivals, our intimate suites are so elegant,

entering our conference rooms,
a meeting is held over intense conference calls; our intimacy is real,
with this corporate merger our shares are sealed.

Our corporate sheets will stay balanced; *Forever*.
This is a magnificent, business *Endeavor*.

No one can purchase our shares; we are the primary share holders;
we will never go *Under*, because this merger is one that was created in the eyes of
the *Beholder*.
Never thinking twice about our corporate plans,
we took out loans and we purchased this land,
managing our debt and strategizing every step; this merger will always be kept.
As we combine our departments, our *Profit Margins* are high, our *Revenues* are high,
and our *Profits* soar through the *Sky*.

We will never sale our institution, it is so costly; something that we can only *Afford*
because we are on one *Accord*.
With our strategic business plan, we will forever monopolize in this land. this is our,
Corporate Merger . . . .

THE EXPLANATION = THE INTERPRETATION: CORPORATE MERGER

This poetic piece is called the Corporate Merger, and it was created for a man to give to his woman, but it can also be a unisex poetic piece. This chapter focuses on the institution of marriage. It explains how two people can come together to form one institution. It is all about marriage, and marriage is an institution that has been around since the beginning of time. This poetic piece uses a business metaphor to explain the institution of marriage. According to Christian tradition, Adam and Eve was the first married couple, and they had a complete union that formed one institution. When men and women decided to take their relationship to the next level, they usually look to get married. When a couple gets married, they also look to start a family; they will start to generate wealth and they are considered to be as one. In a marriage, like a partnership or a joint venture, everything becomes one; both man and woman are united to form one entity, and they are committed to each other. In a marriage, the man and a woman will share their home; their kids; theirs cars, etc. When it comes to marriage, most governments recognize marriage as a union between a man and a woman. A person's spouse can receive the spouse's medical benefits, life insurance, etc. When a spouse dies, the living spouse usually receives their benefits. So, the couple lives as one.

When two people come together and they both decide to get married, they should celebrate the institution. When a man and woman are united in Holy Matrimony; during the marriage ceremony, vows are shared between the man and woman, and there are promises made between the two parties. Likewise, when two business entities come together, both businesses have to abide by bylaws. These bylaws are promises that should be kept while both businesses operate to form one institution. When a man decides to marry a woman, both the man and the woman should have complete trust amongst each other, and they should become one flesh. They should be intimate on different levels, and their love should only be shared amongst each other. While married, the man and the woman should make decisions together that benefit the institution as a whole. There are several key lines in this poetic piece that can be interpreted. The line that says: "our cost analysis will never change," simply means that both the man and the woman should budget their finances and live accordingly to how they choose to live.

When it comes to marriage, both, the man and the woman should work as one, and they should have one heartbeat. According to the Bible and the teachings of Christ, one should leave his or her family and become one flesh with their husband or wife. In Mathew 19.4-6 ESV it states when one of the twelve disciples asked Jesus about marriage, Jesus answered, "Have you not read that who created them from the beginning made them male and woman, and he said, Therefore a man shall leave his father and his mother and hold fast to his wife, and the two shall become one flesh?" So they are no longer two but one Flesh. What therefore God has joined together let not man separated." It is God's divine will that when men and women decides to get married, they leave their mother and father and become one flesh with one another.

Married couples should continue to date and they should make sure that they do the same things that made them fall in love with each other. If couples took long walks in the park before they got married, they should continue to take long walks with each other. There are several situations when couples would date each other for years, then once they decide to get married, they would change their formula which kept them together. Some couples think that once they get married, they should overly indulge in the relationship when they should continue to be the loving couple that they have always been. Couples should continue to romance each other, and they should continue to treat each other as a blessing that God has united.

As the poem states, "our corporate merger has created a superb business relationship with an astonishing sexual relationship, with an extravagant, business intent: All in this Competitive Environment." Couples should understand that there are several things that compete for their love. Children can come in between a couple's love. When couples have children, it's important for the couple to understand that they should keep the relationship alive. Sometimes it's difficult to raise kids, pay bills and have a successful career. In some relationships, kids can become a couple's number one priority, but it's important to love your mate first, and then the couple will both meet each other's needs by providing for the kids. Due to the fact that both, man and the woman love their kids equally, as a unit, the couple will help meet each other's needs when they take care of their children. Sometimes, couples forget that they are in a relationship when they have kids. They focus only on raising their kids, working and paying bills instead of focusing on the romance and the love that brought them together in the first place. It's vital that the man and the women both come together and realize that there are several aspects of competition that takes them away from each other, and their kids can be a form of competition that lures them away from each other.

Friends and family can also be a form of competition. Friends and family can intervene and try to dictate how a marriage institution should be operated. Although, it's always great to get someone's opinion on certain situations about the marriage, but the final decision should be decided between the two CEO's of the marriage institution, which is the husband and the wife. In-laws and best friends always find themselves on the outside looking in a couple's relationship, and they rarely know what's going on with the couple. In-laws and best friends can be detrimental to a marriage. Bad advice can ruin a relationship, and it's important that the married couple communicate with each other and don't get influenced by outsiders. Like each and every corporation, a corporation is different and has its business rules. Likewise, every marriage institution is different, and what works for one marriage may not work for the other marriage. We can use a business analogy to explain this; if Google implements a particular strategy that makes them successful, it doesn't mean that that same business strategy works for Microsoft or Apple.

In a marriage, communication is key, and this is explained in the poem, where it states: "our intimate suites are so elegant as we enter our conference room, a Meeting is held over intense conference calls; our intimacy is real." With this poetic piece, it also states the importance of communication with the statement; "with this corporate merger our shares are sealed;" this statement is intended to explain how intimate conversations are held between a united couple, husband and wife. Also, this line explains how the couple should be primary investors of their relationship. In business, there are situations where a company sells its stocks to the public who will then become shareholders of the business. When a person becomes a shareholder of a particular business, depending on the type of stocks they have purchased, they can dictate how the company is operated. In a marriage, only the man and the woman are the primary shareholders, so, they own all of their stocks; only they can dictate how their marriage is ran, operated and owned. So, that being said; its fine for individuals outside of the marriage to express their opinion, but only the husband and wife should be the ones who run, operate and own the institution. In a marriage, a man and a woman should give all thanks to God. A wife should be recognized as a gift from God, and she should understand that she is the man's soul-help mate. She should be there to support him, and be his helper has he provide for his family. When a woman acts as a helper, she would understand the structure of the family unit. First, God made Adam and then he made Eve. Then between the husband and his wife, out of that union, there came two kids, Cane and Abel. This was the first family, and this is seen in the Biblical verse located below:

When God introduced Adam to his helper, which was Eve, they were one flesh. According to Christian belief, God placed Adam under a deep sleep, and then he created Eve from Adam's rib cage.

In Genesis 2:21-23 (NIV) it states

> "So the Lord God caused the man to fall into a deep
> sleep. While the man slept, the Lord God took out one of the
> man's ribs and closed up the opening. Then the Lord God
> made a woman from the rib, and he brought her to the man.

> After her creation, Adam names his companion Woman,
> at last the man exclaimed, this one is Bone from my Bone,
> and Flesh from my Flesh!
> She will be called "Woman," because she was taken from
> Man.

> This explains why a man leaves his father and mother and
> is joined to his wife, and the two are united into one."

As this poetic piece explains, it's important to ask God for strength while attempting to keep a committed relationship alive; it's important to understand that the marriage institution was created in the eyes of the beholder. Couples should pray together, go to church together and worship the same God, and by doing this, the couple will stay committed to each other. When couples involve God within their marriage, the marriage would be blessed, although there would be trials and tribulations. Sometimes God will put the couple through trials and tribulations to strengthen the marriage. There might be several disagreements, but both the man and the woman should seek God and his word for guidance.

Once a marriage is blessed by God, there would be great gifts that will come from the marriage. Both, the man and the woman will be successful in their careers, and what every they may do, they both will be blessed. As the poem expresses, "or profit margins are high, our revenues are high, and our profits sour through the sky," this simply means that when God blesses this institution, the unit will abundantly be filled with wealth. Both, the man and the woman will find wealth and happiness not only from a monetary standpoint, but both will live in prosperity, and they will have a prosperous life. When God is in control of the marriage, and if the couples seek God, it will be difficult for enemies to infiltrate the marriage unit; both the man and the woman will be able to strategize to create more wealth amongst each other. Together as a unit, the man and woman will have enough income to help provide for their children. This poetic piece ends with the statement: "we will never sale our institution, it is so costly; something that we can only afford because we are one accord." This statement simply means that, marriage should never be broken. This line relates to the classic line, in a wedding ceremony, till death do us part.

Although, it may take some people several times to find their true soul mate, marriage is intended to be a solid institution that stays together until one soul mate leaves this earth. Last but not least, the line that expresses, "with our strategic business plan, we will forever monopolize in this land" simply means that the man and woman should continue to love each other, communicate amongst each other, keep God first, stay equally yoked, and as a unit take care of their children and don't let outsiders influence their God given institution. When this happens, the marriage institution will have the same power as a company that monopolize in its industry. When a company has a monopoly, the company is in its highest position, and it is very difficult to overcome that company. So, when a marriage is blessed by God, and couples create a communication plan and stay equally yoked, the marriage will flourish well beyond expectations.

SECTION V

The Answer—*Trust, Listen, Understand, Believe*

Live happily with the woman you love through all the meaningless days of life that God has given you under the sun. The wife God gives you is your reward for all your earthly toil.

Ecclesiastes 9:9 (NLT)

CHAPTER 15—THE ANSWER

(The relationship Answer for him and her)

YOU ARE

The creator; I was made in your image, but I am simply a mere mortal at the Most.
You send your Angles to protect me from self.
When I was weak, you were the only one who could help.
Preventing me from every unwanted step.
Learning your purpose for my life,
With your unfailing love, you sent your **Son** who paid the ultimate sacrifice.

YOU ARE

My strength, my protection, as I sleep, I awake and you bless me with the ability
To see another day, that's why, each and every day I pray.
I am undeserving of your Grace and Mercy, but you always *Provide*,
In you, I find the strength to *Survive*.

YOU ARE

The light, my hope, my salvation, my complete understanding; when I fall, you
provide your safe landing.

YOU ARE
Deserving of all praise, this World is yours . . . . *Thinking,*
How blessed I am, to be able to experience your gift of *Thanksgiving,*
As I fall short of your will, you said if I confess my wrong doings with my heart,
you will always be *Forgiving.*

This is the POWER of your LOVE!!

YOU ARE
The Beginning and the End, Alpha and Omega, the Founder of all Nations, the
Creator of all Knowing;
The creator of Time, the source of All Mankind, **YOU ARE**, The Earth's deepest
Ocean,
The Earth's highest Mountain, every Valley and every Peak belongs to your Holy
Name,
When my enemies attack me, you blanket me with a thick Mane,
You always protect me from their burning Flame.

YOU ARE Eternity; **YOU ARE** the only food source for ME.
You will never leave or forsake me.
That's why you are . . . . the ALMIGHTY!!

THE EXPLANATION = THE INTERPRETATION: YOU ARE

How do we truly find our ideal soul-mate? Well this chapter provides the answer to this question. Usually, men and women try to search for love, but they should seek God and wait for God to send them their ideal soul-mate. Whether it's a man or a woman, it's best **not** to search for love, but let **love find you** and stay focus on the one who created you, God. If you stay focused on the creator, and improve your character, your self-esteem as well as your self-assurance, God will send you your ideal mate. Whether you are a male or female, you should always keep a positive attitude and a positive outlook on life. When this happens, your ideal soul-mate will walk into your life. If men and women stay patient and focused, whether it's straightening out their credit, focus on their career, build a better relationship with God and address issues in their personal life, it would be easy for them to find their ideal soul-mate. For example, if a woman works to maintain her weight, and she keeps a positive outlook on life, dresses nice, keeps her hair done, works to improve her financial situation, and she continues to grow in Christ, God will send her the man of her dreams without her even knowing it.

If women stay focus on God, and improve their woman hood status, men will flock to them, but it's important to stay mindful of these men, because ultimately God gives men and women free will to choose who we want to be with. So, we must be diligent in God's word and choose someone who is equally yoked. Sometimes God places our ideal mate in front of us, but we will turn this mate away. For example, a woman might meet her soul-mate, but because her standards are too high, this woman misses out on that man. Sometimes, a woman may give up on love when they experience a bad relationship instead of being patient and let God send her ideal soul-mate. A woman might have to wait longer than usual for her ideal man, but when he walks in her life, it would be worth the wait. While waiting for the ideal man, women should continue to work on self-improvement, and when this man comes, she would be surprised as to how she met him. Likewise, men should also understand, if God is sought out first, then, if he continues to build his character and self-assurance, there would be no problem finding his ideal woman.

Understand and Overcome Stubbornness

God intended for man to have a wife, and he created a woman to be his helper. Men, we should understand that we should cherish our woman and treat her like the gift that she is. Men should understand that a woman has a role to play in their lives. Men, we should always remember: as a woman grows breast and feed a child, she has an intuition that enables her to be a help-mate. Men, sometimes we have to let go of our pride and let our woman whom God placed in our lives, help us. We can be very stubborn when it comes to a woman's help, and it's important for women to understand the stubbornness of a man. Woman should continue to support their man when she is in a relationship and when necessary, let him make his decisions because men and women think differently. It's important to understand a man's decisions can be, and should be inspired by a woman. Likewise, when women make decisions, those decisions can also be inspired by her man. While in a relationship, men should let his woman motivate him, and both, men and women should be grateful that God sent that particular person in their life. So, it's important not to take that person for granted.

Trust and Overcome Temptation

Trust, listen, and seek God and love will follow!! God speaks to men and women several different ways. Men and women should understand, when it comes to a relationship, we can battle and overcome temptation. If the cheating man wants to change his cheating ways, but he struggles, he should seek strength from a higher power, God. God is all knowing, and he knows how many strands of hair that we have on our head; he understands our battles and he can help us overcome our temptations. When men seek God, he will always have enough money to provide for his family. To provide for his family, a man may not have his ideal job, but God will always place him within reach of some type of income that will help him support and provide for his family. Men should keep faith, and learn how to deal with trials and tribulations and all of the sexual temptations that he may face while being in a committed relationship.

When a man's flesh is weak, and he has the lust of the eye, he should lean on God for strength. When men and women are successful, and they are madly in love, they both become instant targets for temptation. In a relationship, a man and a woman should both place their mates on a peddle stool; men should treat his woman like the gift that she is, and women should treat their man like the king that he is. Once this happens, God will provide the strength to battle temptation. Men, when there is an opportunity to cheat, it might not be worth it to sleep with another woman and jeopardize your relationship. Before cheating, it's always important to understand that God sends a woman to a man to help him build a home. It may not be worth it to step out of your committed relationship and risk losing everything because of a home wrecker. Ladies, it's also important to seek God when battling temptation. You should make sure that you recognize when you are being lured away from your man. As mentioned earlier in this book, the grass is not always greener on the other side, and leaving a good man for a falsified man is never a good thing.

When it comes to cheating, everyone is human and everyone makes mistakes. When a man or a woman find themselves in situations where there is an opportunity to cheat, and the cheating act occurs, God chastises us. We will start to feel guilty about cheating, but we should recognize that we make mistakes, and its best to learn from our mistakes. Men, when we cheat, we should always remember, what comes around, goes around, and if our woman cheats, it hurts twice as bad because when she cheats, it hurts our pride. Men, it may be very tempting not to sleep with other women, but if we approach cheating as if we were cheating on God, instead of cheating on our woman, it will be easy to overcome any cheating ways.

Women, when a man cheats, and if he is truly sorry for his cheating, you should fully forgive him. You can forgive, but not forget, and based off of the situation, you can either stay with him or decide to leave him. It's always important to remember, if God can forgive, so can we. If you express that you forgive your man for cheating, you should completely forgive him. You shouldn't constantly bring up the cheating episode. Although it is wrong to cheat, women must understand that everyone makes mistakes; Ladies, when you say that you fully forgive someone, you should truly forgive. When men and women live accordingly to God's plan, and they are happy, the Devil will attempt to do everything to break up the union, but it's important that couples stay strong and don't fall victim to temptation.

Listen and Believe

When there are problems in a relationship, it's important to stay patient, pray and ask God for guidance. When a man and a woman don't stay together, sometimes it is God's plan for that relationship not to survive. Men and women should listen to God, and let him speak to their hearts about the one whom is right for them. Relationships are like a job, and before a person take a new position for a job, it's best to pray and ask God for his blessing. This same ideology should be taken when someone thinks about pursuing a full committed relationship. While dating, men and women frequently fail to pay attention to the signs of their potential mate; they ignore all the negative aspects of that person. For example, men and women would date certain people and ignore all of the signs that express that this person is not a good match. People would overlook a person's baggage and their troubling issues because they desperately want to be in a relationship. When dating, people usually date a person's representative for the first three months, and once their representative leaves, the real person shows up. Once this real person shows up, they might have issues that may be very difficult to deal with. When we are dating, it is on the job training, and after three months of probation, there may be signs in the relationship that explains how the couple may not be equally yoked.

God speaks to us in several different ways, and he protects us by sending us subliminal messages about certain individuals who are not a good fit for our life. God speaks to us by giving us signs and clues that an individual is not our ideal mate. For example, if a woman is involved with a man, but she is not sure about being with that man because of his bad habits, God will make his bad behaviors intensify, ultimately giving the woman the choice to choose if she want to continue dating him or not. When we are in abusive relationships, ultimately, we can choose to walk away or stay. God will give us several opportunities to leave that person. In a relationship, there also may be compatibility issues between the couple. For example, if a person starts a new job, knowing that that job is not right for them, they would be miserable at that job. That person might not be a good fit for that job, and the compatibility issues may cause all types of problems for both, the employee and the employer. God will let us choose to stay with an individual that is not compatible with us because he gives us free will. Due to us having free will, God will send us warning signs about that person, and it all depends on us to decide if we want to stay with a certain individual or not. In some instances, people will marry someone for the wrong reasons, and they will find themselves miserable because that person was not the right match. When someone is "crazy," or not the right match, God would let us know, but it's up us to choose to stay with that person or not.

Both, men and women make major mistakes by not listening to God when he shows us the signs that our mate is not right for us. Women fall victim to this all the time because they are afraid of being along. When a man constantly cheats on a woman, constantly uses her, and constantly degrade her; women should understand that she is in an awkward position. Some women fall into the ***"I am in Love Trap."*** Because women are emotional creatures, it may be difficult for them to walk away from an abusive relationship. Some women may not realize that if they decide to leave this abusive man, the man of her dreams may be waiting for her. This concept also applies to the man as well. Likewise, a man may be in an abusive relationship with a woman who sleeps around, or keep up havoc and drama. This woman may also be a gold digger who only wants to be with this man because of his money. So, not only should the woman recognize the signs of an abusive relationship, men should too. Again, when a mate lacks compatibility, God will intensify their behaviors, making it easy for a man or a woman to recognize that person's issues.

Communication is very important in a relationship. It's vital to listen and speak about things that are not going right within a relationship, and if that relationship cannot be prepared, it may be best for the couple to go their separate ways. In this instance, God's purpose may be to put you through a bad relationship to better help you with your next relationship. Love is very essential to every committed relationship, and companionship is equally important. It's vital that men and women understand that temptations will be present when you find the one that is right for you. When there are problems in the relationship, it's important to explore every possible avenue to keep the relationship alive, but if that relationship doesn't work, it just doesn't work. While dating, it's always important to make sure that that person is equally yoked. Men and women should understand that God always has a plan for their life, and each and every person can find love, but its best to wait on God; work on self-improvement and be patient and let God send you your true love.

"The Relationship Guide to make him or her commit"

SECTION VI

Learn his sport in Plain English

The Woman's Sports Cheat Sheet
(Football, Basketball, Baseball)

MEN AND THEIR SPORTS
(WHAT'S THE BIG DEAL?)

Men usually love sports, and it would be great if women also learn how to enjoy sports. Woman, if you don't like sports, don't worry because this will not make or break your relationship, but if you learn to like your man's sport, he will be more likely to commit to you, especially if he is a huge sports fan. If a woman doesn't like sports, again, this will not make or break your relationship; women, you should understand that sports are soap operas for men, and that's why we enjoy watching sports. Although you can view sports as being soap operas, sports are not fictional. The athletes are real people, and the game is real. When women nag their man because he watches sports, it's never a good idea. Men enjoy sports because they are competitive creatures. Men love to bet on sporting events, and when they win, they not only receive money, they receive bragging rights. Women make the major mistakes when they try to sex their man while he is watching a good game, and when you are turned down, you feel neglected. Women, if you just wait until the game goes off, and then ask for the sex, your man would make great love to you especially if his team wins. Women, you should become a sports fan, and the best way to do this is to have a favorite team. If your man is an advocate sports fan, once in his life, he may have wanted to play sports. Professional athletes make millions of dollars and they are very famous. Professional sports can be an escape for men, and although some men will not admit it, when their women are also sports fans, the woman would gain extra commitment points from their man. For men, it's a great experience if his woman enjoys sports. Sports are a form of entertainment, and it's a great social event. Men talk about sports amongst peers, and if a woman can be that man's friend and talk about sports with him, she would gain commitment points.

Most women don't like to watch sports because they simply don't understand the game. Once you understand the game, you would understand how important it is to your man!!! For example, football is interesting because it's more than just the hard hits and the funny dances in the End Zone; it's about out thinking your opponent. Men enter Fantasy Football Leagues that earn them money, and they usually enter weekly football pools at work. With Fantasy Football Leagues and the football pools, men can win hundreds of dollars on a weekly basis. Men also love football because football games are usually played once a week, but there may be the occasional game on Thursday or Saturday. In football, a team can beat another team by simply running the ball or throwing the ball, or the team can win with a winning field goal. Women should understand that it's better for their man to be in front of a TV screen instead of some Sweaty Strip Club!!

Sports can be a great social event for both, men and women. The four main sports that men enjoy are: Football, Basketball, Baseball, and Hockey. Men also enjoy watching highlights from each sport. TV shows, such as Sport Center replay all the best highlights from previous games. Highlights can be the best passes of the day, the best runs of that day, the best dunks of the day, or simply the best plays that happened in the game. For the male sport's fan, it varies on which sport is his favorite. Women, your man might not be into any of the four sports listed above; he might be into MA Fighting, Tennis, Golf, NASCAR Racing or Boxing. Sports are a lot of fun, and sport athletes appear to have super human capabilities. Women, it's important to keep sports simple, and try to learn your man's sport and as a couple, you both can enjoy the game!!!

FOOTBALL CHEAT SHEET FOR WOMEN

Women, the best way to learn football is to look at the sport as a woman trying to reach her man that has a pot of gold at the end of 100 yards, and once she reaches these 100 yards, she will obtain this pot of gold and her man will become her sex slave. With this analogy, a man gives a woman a ball, and with this ball, the woman can walk or run 100 yards to get this ball to him while he is standing in the End Zone. The woman will have 4 chances to get 100 yards, with increments of 10 yards. Every time she gets 10 yards, she gets 4 more chances to get another 10 yards until she reaches 100 yards. At the end of the 100 yards, her man stands in the End Zone waiting to give her his pot of gold, and he awaits for her, wanting to become her Sex Slave. So, if the woman move 10 yards, she has 90 more to yards to go until she gets to the End Zone. If she moves 10 more yards, she has 80 more yards to go until she gets to the End Zone. If she moves 10 more yards, she only has 70 more yards to go until she gets into the End Zone. Once the woman has walked or ran all 100 yards, she will reach the End Zone and she will score a Touchdown.

Women, while using this analogy, in football there are challenges when it comes to getting the ball to your man. Let us say, there is another woman who also want to get the ball to her man, and this other woman has to run in the opposite direction to reach her man. So, this other woman wants to stop you from reaching your man, and she will try everything possible to stop you from reaching your man. The first woman who reaches their man scores a touchdown and the game is over. (This is basically the game of Football, but in the real game of Football, upon receiving a Touchdown, the game is not over, it all depends on who has the highest score at the end of 4 regulated quarters. There are 4, 15 minute quarters in football, and the team that has the highest score wins the game.)

Ladies, in football, each team may throw the ball or run the ball to get to the End Zone, and once you reach the End Zone, you score a "Touchdown." Using the above analogy, again, once the woman get the ball to her man, the woman will score a touchdown. Let's also say once she reaches the End Zone, she also obtains a pot of gold from her man, and once she receives this pot of gold, she can do whatever she wants with this money. She can buy clothes, a house, or whatever she wants. Remember, the woman moves in increments of 10 until she reaches 100 yards until she get into the End Zone.

What does 1ˢᵗ, 2ⁿᵈ, 3ʳᵈ and 4ᵗʰ down mean?

The down system is explained:
Steps are used instead of yards for simplicity

1ˢᵗ Down: In football, the object is to gain 100 steps, using 4 chances. In football, there will be 4 chances, and the first chance is called the 1ˢᵗ down. With the first down, using the analogy mentioned earlier in this **Sports Guide for Woman**, if you try to get to your man by reaching the End Zone, and there is another woman who tries to stop you, you only have 4 tries, and again, your first try will be the 1ˢᵗ down. In football, the other woman will try to take the ball away from you because she wants to run the ball in the opposite direction to get to her man. If you, as the main women move 3 steps, and the other woman stops you, you will have 3 more tries to get to your man in the End Zone. As you gain steps, your steps are totaled until the entire steps equal 10. In this case, you have only moved a **TOTAL of 3 steps**.

In football, the team moves in 10 step increments until 100 yards are reached. This may sound complicated, but woman once you watch the game, it makes perfect since. Once you watch a football game on television, the television would have a yellow line that shows how far a player has to go to reach 10 steps, and once the player reaches 10 steps, he has 4 more tries to get another 10 steps. Once the player get 10 more steps, he gets 4 more tries to get another 10 steps. Then, once he gets

10 more steps, he gets 4 more tries to get another 10 steps. This process repeats itself until the man reaches the End Zone and scores a Touch Down. Ladies, remember if you are on defense, the object of the game is to STOP the man from getting 10 steps, and stop him from getting into the End Zone.

2nd Down: Going back to the woman's analogy, on your 2nd attempt, you move **3 more steps**, and know you have a **Total of 6 steps**, but you need a **Total of 10 steps.** So, in this case because you acquired 3 steps, you have 4 more steps until you get a Total of 10 steps, but because this is the 2nd down, you only have 2 more tries: **3rd down and 4th down.** If you get all ten steps, you get 4 more tries to get another 10 steps, and this process repeats until the entire steps equal 100.

Ladies to make football clear and easy, remember, in football, men try to move the ball in increments of 10 until they reach 100 steps. As a player in this football analogy, you/as the main woman desperately wants your man's pot of gold, but to get to your man, you have to get past this other woman and she tries everything to stop you from getting to your man. On your 2nd down/ your second chance, the other woman keeps trying to hold you back, and she desperately want the ball from you because she wants to run the opposite direction to get to her man. If on your 2nd attempt, the other woman stops you, you will be given a 3rd chance to get a **Total of 10 steps**, and move to another 10 step increment. Remember, you are moving in increments of 10 until you reach 100 steps to get into the End Zone. Your man awaits you, and her man awaits her. (Ladies, this is the game of Football, WHO WILL WIN THEIR MAN??)

3rd Down: This is your 3rd chance to get the first increment of 10 steps, and you only have a total of **6 steps**, but you need 4 more steps to get a total of 10. On your first try (1st down), you only walked 3 steps. On your second try (2nd down) you only walked 3 more steps, so on both of these tries, your steps total to **6 steps**. If you get 4 more steps, you will reach the first 10 step increment, and then you will get 4 more tries to get another 10 steps. Remember you gain increments of 10 until you reach 100 steps. When you get 100 steps, you are in the End Zone, and you will have a Touchdown. You will win your man, and his pot of gold becomes yours and he becomes your sex slave. Ladies, remember, when watching the game, there will always be a posting telling you what down it is and how far a football member has to go until they get into the End Zone.

4th Down: Ladies, if you need 4 tries to get into the End Zone, you must remember this is your last and final try to get to your man's pot of gold, or at least get a total of 10 steps. If you get the 10 steps, you will have 4 more tries to either get another 10 steps, and these 10 step increments continue until the steps Total 100.

The Football Scenario-the Downs

Ladies, let's say on 4th down, which would be your last and final try to either get 10 more yards or get a touchdown. You need 99 steps/yards to reach your End Zone, but you only need 1 step to get your first increment of 10 steps. The other woman thinks very hard to try to take the ball from you, and she stops you from walking or running the final step; now you have to give her your ball, and you have to try to stop her from getting to her man because you failed to get one measly step!! If you would have gotten past this woman, and earned 1 step, you would have at least gotten 4 more tries to get another 10 steps, but you blew it and you failed to get the 1 step. Now, because you blew it, you have to give her the ball. It hurts because once you turn the ball over to her, you fail to stop her and she reaches her man, and you lose the game. Not only do you lose the game, all of your girlfriends whom were cheering for you are very upset because you could not get one measly step, which cost you the game. In real life football, situations similar to this always happen, and a team has to explain why they could not get one measly step to win the game, upsetting millions of football fans.

Now, let us say, on your last and final down, which would be the 4th down, you run past this other woman, and you not only get the 1 measly step, but you run past her, and you run the full 99 steps until you reach your man. As a football player, you did not need an extra increment of 10 steps because you out smarted this other woman and you reached the End Zone. Once you reached **the** End Zone, you score a **Touch Down!!** You have just SCORED a TOUCHDOWN!!!! On your last and final try, you ran 99 steps/yards to reach your man!!! You have won your MAN, and your girlfriends love you because they are very excited for you!! You **CELEBRATE**, and they **CELEBRATE** with you!! You are happy that you won the game because you reached your Man!! Upon reaching him, he becomes your Sex Slave; he makes love to and you have multiple orgasms!! After you have multiple orgasms, he gives you his pot of gold, and he takes you shopping. You also find out that his pot of gold is worth 100 million dollars, and you can spend the remaining dollars however you choose. The other woman or the HEFFA who tried to stop you is feeling very upset and she is crying because she could not stop you from getting to your MAN!! She had 4 chances to stop you, but she could not hold you back on your final and last down. As a lady, because you scored a Touch Down, you won the game!! Again, the MAN takes you out, become your Sex Slave, buy you elegant meals, spend millions of dollars on you, and take you home and make sweet passionate love to you!!

Football Terms: continued

Turn Over on Downs: When this happens, you failed to get a touchdown or you failed to get 10 steps using your 4 tries. The other woman gains control of the ball, and now, you have to try to stop this HEFFA from getting to her man!! Like you, she has 4 attempts to get a touchdown, and when she scores a touchdown the game is over, but in the real game of football, the other team just has a chance to score the football. The game is over after time has passed, and whichever team has the highest score wins.

Number of Steps/Yards: Ladies, in football, there are 100 steps, and there are four chances to get 10 steps. When watching football on TV, there will always be a yellow line that tells how far a player has to go until they can get 4 more chances to get 10 yards or score a Touchdown. When men watch the game, they rely on this yellow line to let then know how far their team has to go until the team has reached the first down.

This yellow line is called the "First Down Marker." In football, you will see something like, "1st and 10." This means that this is your first try to get 10 steps. Then you might see "2nd and 8." This means this is your second try to get eight steps. Then you might see "3rd and 2." This means that this is your third try to get two steps. On 3rd and 2, if you get the 2 steps, the count start back over, and it would be "1st and 10." This process repeats itself until you reach your man in the End Zone and score a Touchdown.

10 steps = 4 attempts. 4 attempts = 10 steps. The process repeats itself until the team reaches the End Zone and scores a Touchdown.

Football Offence in Plain English (11 men on the field)

Offence—This is when the team has the ball and the team tries to move down the field attempting to get closer and closer to the End Zone and score a *Touchdown.*

Quarterback—The man who either throws the ball to his players or hand the ball off to his players. The Quarterback is usually the Team Captain. Patton Manning plays the Quarterback position, Michael Vick plays the Quarterback position and Tom Brady also plays the Quarterback position.

Running Back—The man who runs the ball. He can be a fat running man or a normal size running man. These players might be the fastest players on the football field. Walter Payton was a known running back. Most men compare today's running backs to the great, late Walter Payton. Ladies, Barry Sanders, Emit Smith and Marshal Faulk are all well known running backs as well.

Wide Receivers—This is the man who catches the ball after the Quarterback throws the ball to him. After the Wide Receiver catches the ball, he will keep running until he is tackled by the opposing team. If the Wide Receiver is not tackled, he will run until he reaches the End Zone for 6 points. Once he enters the End Zone, this player scores a Touchdown, and the player would usually do a funny looking dance, and men will either celebrate or get mad when this player enters the End Zone for 6 points. Randy Moss is a profound Wide Receiver. Amongst the football league, Terrell Owens is a known wide receiver, and Jerry Rice is also a known Wide Receiver.

Tight End—This man usually catches the ball, and he is an offensive player. Ladies, remember when a player is on offence, his team is trying to score the ball. They are trying to run or throw the ball until they reach the End Zone. The Tight End is slightly bigger and stronger than the usual Wide Receiver.

Offensive Linemen or Offensive Line—6 fat men that protect the man who throws the ball, whom is the Quarterback. The offensive linemen also block for the guy who runs the ball, whom is the Running Back. If the Quarterback decides not to throw the ball to a Wide Receiver, he can hand the ball to the Running Back or toss it to him. The Quarterback might even keep the ball and run the ball himself. When this happens, men go crazy because the Quarterback usually does not run the ball because he is prone to injury. Michael Vick is a quarterback that is known for running the ball. The Offensive line will protect the Running Back, Wide Receivers and/or the Quarterback as well as the Tight End until one of these players get into the End Zone and score a Touchdown.

Football Defense in Plain English *(11 men on the field)*

Defense—These are the men whom try to stop the opposing team from reaching the End Zone. Each and every player who is designated to play defense must try to stop the opposing team from reaching the End Zone.

Defensive Line—These are the fat guys on the field who tackles the Quarterback and other players on the football field. When the Quarterback gets tackled by one of these big fat guys, the big fat guy has Sacked the Quarterback. After a Sack, the big fat guy, usually a Defensive lineman, will due a funny looking dance or a funny gesture. When a Sack occurs, men will usually cheer or scream at the game. When a Sack occurs, it all depends on the team your man is rooting for, your man will be either upset or he will be very happy. If your man is a fan of the Defensive Lineman who Sacked the quarterback, your man would be very excited. A Quarterback should never get Sacked in the game of football, but ladies it does happen. To avoid a sack, Quarterbacks should hurry up and throw the ball to one of his players.

Corner Back—In football, these are the guys who play on the defensive side of the ball. Remember ladies, in football, there are players who try to stop a player from scoring, and they play on defense. The players who try to score the ball are on the offense, and again, the Corner Backs are players who play on the defensive side of the ball because they try to stop the opposing team from catching the ball. These guys are the smaller guys on the football field. Ladies, every player in football are not big fat guys; the Corner Backs are the size of track stars, and they are usually muscular built. They are smaller built guys because they do a lot of running. Deon "Prime Time" Sanders was a profound Corner Back in his day.

Safety—smaller guys that also try to stop the Wide Receivers from catching the ball, after the quarterback throws the ball. These guys also play on the defensive side of the ball. Ladies, every player in football is not a big fat guy, and these guys are the size of track stars, and they are muscular built. They are smaller built guys because they do a lot of running.

Middle Line Backer—These are the players on defense that protect the middle of the field. Remember ladies, if we are using the woman analogy, if you are on defense, you are trying to stop your woman from going into the End Zone, and if you were a Middle Linebacker, you would protects the middle of the field. If the Quarterback throws this ball in your direction, you should try your best to knock the ball out of a Wide Receiver's hand. If a quarterback throws the ball in the middle of the field, and a Wide Receiver catches the ball, as a Middle Line Backer, you would usually be the first to hit the Wide Receiver; trying to make him drop the ball. Ladies, football is a contact sport, and the object is to not let your opponent catch or run the ball into their End Zone for a Touchdown.

Keeping the Score

Touchdown—This is when either team enters the End Zone

End Zone = **6 points**—To get into the End Zone is the entire objective of the game. Both teams try to get into the End Zone, and when a player gets into the End Zone, they will **score 6 points** for their Team. This is when men shout and go crazy because this is the entire point of the game.

Field Goal—The big yellow post in the End Zone

Field Goal Kick/ Extra Point =**1 point**—One point after team scores a Touchdown

Field Goal Kick = **3 points**—If a team can't get a touchdown, they would usually kick a Field Goal. Men scream and shout if a kicker kicks a long Field Goal to win the Game. If the Kicker is close enough to kick the Field Goal, and he fail to kick the ball thru the big yellow posts, guys would shout at the TV or at the Game.

***2 Point Conversion* = 2 points**—This is when the team wants to throw or run the ball into the End Zone instead of kicking a Field Goal. If the team decides to throw the ball or run the ball into the End Zone after a Touchdown, the team gets 2 points instead of a 1 point Field Goal. Teams usually would kick a 1 point field goal because it is easier to kick the 1 point Field Goal instead of trying to run the ball or throw the ball for a two point conversion.

***Safety* = 2 points**—Ladies, the best way is to look at a safety is to look at it as a reverse Touchdown. To get a safety, the team must have possession of the ball, but they get tackled in the opposite End Zone. If players go forward and they have the ball and reaches the End Zone, it's a Touchdown, but when they go backwards and they have the ball and get tackled in the opposite End Zone, it's called a Safety.

Punter—This is the man who kicks the ball to the other team after his team either scores a touchdown or his team fails to score a touchdown. After a Touchdown, the other team has to give the ball to the opposing team, and they kick or punt the ball to them.

Onside Kick—This is when the Punter/ Kicker acts like he is going to kick the ball far down the field, but he tricks the opposing team by kicking the ball 10 yards giving his team a high advantage to get the ball back after it is kicked.

Loosing Yards or Giving the Ball to the Other Team

Loosing Yards/ Lost of Yards—In football, the object of the game is to move forward, but due to penalties or being tackled, a team can move backwards. Moving backwards makes it difficult to obtain the full 100 yards needed to get a Touch Down. When a player makes his team move backwards because he committed a dumb play or a foul, men scream at the TV, they scream at the Game; they may scream at the Referee or they may scream at the player who commits the mistake. Once a foul is committed, the Referee will tell what player made the dumb mistake and the Referee will also say how many backwards steps the team has to take.

Sack—This is when one of the guys from the other team tackles the Quarterback while the Quarterback is moving backwards.

Fumble—This is when a player looses the ball. When this happens, the player may give the ball to the other players on the opposite team. When a fumble occurs, the man who fumbled the ball might get the ball back or his team members may recover the ball.

Interception—This is when the Quarterback throws the ball to the opposite team, instead of throwing it to his team mate. The Quarterback never tries to do this, but he does make mistakes. When a Quarterback throws an interception, it's not always his fault; it may be his dumb Wide Receiver's fault for not catching the ball. Men scream at the TV or the game when this happens. They may also scream at players or at the game when an interception is thrown.

Other things to know in Football

How many quarters in Football?—In football, there are 4 quarters, 15 minute each

How many games in a Season?—As of 2012, each football team plays a total of 17 games

How often do Teams Play?—Once a week

How many teams enter the Playoffs?—12 of the best teams

How many teams in the Professional Football League?—As of 2012, 32 Teams

What is the Pro Bowl?—This is when the best players compete against each other; they all *get together and play a game*

BASKETBALL CHEAT SHEET FOR WOMEN

Ladies, basketball is very simple, and it is not like football. Once in their life, men have wished that they could have been a professional basketball player. When a player plays in the National Basketball Association (NBA), he usually makes millions of dollars. Men may watch basketball because they have a favorite team, and each basketball team is different. Ladies, men love basketball because on every play, they can scream at the TV or at the Game. Basketball has several highlights, and basketball has a lot of stupid players who cause stupid plays. These stupid players drive men crazy. Ladies, men also watch basketball because of the fouls committed by other players. Fouls are very important because once a player picks up 6 fouls; he no longer can play the game. When players foul other players, a foul can alter the shot of another player, and when this happens, men scream at the TV or scream at the game. In basketball, there are several awesome players who can score the ball in unbelievable ways. Once these players display their unbelievable talents, men scream at the TV or scream at the game. In basketball, some players make other players look very stupid, and it can be very humorous when an awesome player scores on a not so talented player. In basketball, coaches may also make stupid plays because they control when a player plays in the game. A basketball player does not dictate if he plays in a game or not; it all depends on the player's coach.

A basketball team usually has a roster of 12 players. Ladies, basketball is a team sport, and the 5 best players on a basketball team are called the basketball "Starting Lineup." Basketball is all about scoring the basketball, and trying to stop the other players from scoring the basketball. To score the basketball, each player has a position to play. The player's positions consist of players being tall to short. The taller you are, the easiest it should be to score the basketball, but this is not always the case. If a tall player scores easily, the basketball coach from the opposing team will tell one of his tall players to guard the other tall player. Basketball relies on endurance, and it is a very fatigue sport. Basketball relies on the conditioning of players, and players can get tired very quickly if they are not in the best physical shape. A basketball coach has to decide what players they should play to give his team the best chances to win. To better understand basketball, its best to know the positions players play on the court.

The Starting Lineup: (from Tall to Short)

Center—This is usually the tallest man on the court. He usually will stand near the basket. This will be someone like the great Hall of Famer and five time NBA Champion, Shaquille (SHAQ) O'Neal. In SHAQ's playing days, he was listed as 7 feet tall, and he weighed 320 pounds. When a man plays the center position, he would usually wait until one of the smaller players give him the ball, and he will dunk the ball or easily lay the ball into the basket. He may also shoot the ball depending on the situation.

Power Forward—This person is usually the second tallest person on the court. The Power Forward is big, and he doesn't stand that far from the basket ball hoop. He is a tall person, but he is more agile than the center. The best known Power Forwards are Charles Barkley, Karl Malone, Tim Duncan and Kevin Garnett.

Small Forward—This person is the third tallest person on the basketball court. The Small Forward can shoot the ball; he is more agile than the Power Forward and the Center. This person can play multiple positions on the basketball court because he is the third tallest person on the court. This person can usually run fast, shoot the ball, dunk the ball and play great defense. The most known Small Forwards who played in the NBA are Scottie Pippen, Lamar Odem and the future NBA Hall of Famer, Labron James.

Shooting Guard—This is the fourth tallest person on the court. This person usually scores a lot of the team's points. This person is usually the best scorer on the basketball team, but each team has their unique shooting guard. Some shooting guards will just shoot three pointers, or they may be there to just play great defense. The most prominent Shooting Guards are the future NBA Hall of Famer, Kobe Bryant and 6 time NBA Champion, Michael Jordan.

Point Guards—This is the fifth tallest person on the court, but in some cases, these players can also be as tall as a Shooting Guard or a Small Forward. The responsibility of a Point Guard is to get everyone involved into the game. The Point Guard makes sure that he gets his team mates in the best position to score the basketball. The most prominent Point Guards were the 5 time NBA Champion, Magic Johnson, and NBA Hall of Famers, Isaiah Thomas and John Stockton.

Women, when watching basketball, all of the members will pass the ball to each other until the best possibilities of scoring the ball are reached. The Point Guard's primary job is to dribble the basketball up the court and pass the ball to other team members enabling them to score a basket. There are some scoring point guards who pass the ball and be prominent scorers. Magic Johnson was one of these point guards. As of 2013, Derrick Rose of the Chicago Bulls and Russell Westbrook of the Oklahoma Thunder are both point guards who can easily score the ball and pass the ball.

Things to know in Basketball

Foul—Ladies, in basketball, men watch something that is called a foul. Once a player has the ball, he can't be aggressively touched by a defensive player. Once the player has the ball and he is aggressively touched, it may alter his shot. A foul can also be considered as: aggressive pushing, holding, illegal use of hands, hand checking, illegal use of elbows and of course if someone is fighting.

Flagrant Foul—This is when a player hits another player upside the head. Any player who commits two flagrant fouls will be thrown out of the game.

How Many Fouls does a player need to Foul Out of the Game?—A player needs 6 fouls to foul out of the game. When a player Fouls Out, he can no longer play in the game.

Dribble the Ball—This is when a man bounces the ball up and down and run around the court

Dunk the Ball—This when a player place the ball in the basket while touching the basket's rim

Assist—This is when a player past the ball to his teammate and his teammate scores the ball. The person who passes the ball receives an assists.

Triple Double—This is when a player receives at least, 10 points, 10 rebounds and 10 assists.

Double Double—This is when a player receives a total of 10 or stats for two of the three categories mentioned above in the triple double definition. For example, a player can have 10 points and 10 rebounds. Once a player receives these stats, he would have recorded a Double Double for that game.

Rebound—This is when the ball hits the rim after someone shoots the ball, and a basketball player from either team grabs the ball.

Three Point Shot—This is when players shoot the ball behind the white line.

Charge/Offensive Foul—This is when a player dribbles the ball into a player, but the defending player's feet must be in a squared position.

How Many Quarters is it in Basketball?—There are usually 4 quarters, 12 minutes each

What is a Shot Clock?—In the NBA, this is the clock that is on top of the basketball goal. A team has 24 seconds to shoot the ball, and if the team does not score a basket within these 24 seconds, they turn the ball over to the opposing team. Men scream at the TV or at the game when a team fails to get a shot off within the boundaries of 24 seconds.

Other things to know in Basketball

How many quarters in Basketball?—In basketball, there are 4 quarters, 12 minute each

How many games in a Basketball Season?—As of 2012, each basketball team plays a total of 81 games

How many teams enter the Basketball Playoffs?—16 of the best teams

How many teams in the National Basketball League?—30 Teams

What is the All Star Game—this is when the best players compete against each other, they all get together and play a game.

Reasons why men shout and cheer during the Game (NOTE: Ladies, when it comes to screaming at the game, it's best not to over emphasize cheering or screaming because all the excessive screaming may become annoying to your man, especially if you shout at the Game for no reason)

1.) When a favorite player gets fouled and the referee does not call the foul, causing your favorite player to miss his shot
2.) When a player misses an open shot or an easy layup
3.) When a player fail to catch the ball, causing the ball to go out of bounds
4.) When a person gets dunk on or when a person performs an awesome dunk
5.) If a person cannot stop another person from scoring
6.) If a coach take a player out of the game when the player has a hot scoring streak (why would a coach do this? This is what men would usually say!!)
7.) When a player hits a ridiculous shot or when a player hits a shot to win the game
8.) When a player steals the ball from another player
9.) When players get fouled very hard and they start fighting
10.) When a player dives on the ground to get the ball
11.) When a team fails to score within 24 seconds of the shot clock
12.) When a player keeps trying to score the basketball when he knows he can not shoot the ball
13.) When a player over look better players on his team and decides not to pass the ball, causing the opposing team get more shot opportunities
14.) When a team lacks effort and they play slow and sluggish
15.) When a player is just PLAIN STUPID!!!

BASEBALL CHEAT SHEET FOR WOMEN

Baseball is the oldest professional sport in America. Men love baseball because of its historic nature, and it is considered to be a leisure sport. Men love to barbeque and drink beer and watch this sport. In baseball, a baseball player can make more money than any other professional sport in the world. For example, in 2012, Albert Pujos of signed a 10 year 240 million dollar contract to play with the Los Angeles Angels. Like football, there is a defensive team and there is an offensive team. One team plays offense and one team plays defense. When a player is playing defense, the baseball player tries to get the offensive team out. When a player plays offense, the player tries to score a run. Baseball is one of the sports that do not have a time clock. The object of the game is to play 9 innings, and after the 9 innings, the team with the highest score wins the game.

In baseball, there are 9 defensive field positions. Each position is played to stop the opposing team from scoring a run. Baseball has its strategies and its unique highlights, but it is a long game. In baseball, there are 162 games and every game counts. It is a very intriguing sport, and there are millions of baseball fans throughout the world. Baseball is America's most beloved summer sport. In baseball, a highlight might be when a man hit the ball and run to first base, or when a double play occurs. A double play is when there are two outs within one single play. Men watch baseball because of the homeruns, the many highlights, the double and triple plays, the baseball rivalries amongst teams and the baseball strategies each team uses to win the game. Baseball usually is judged by the team who commit the least amount of "Errors." It is unlike any other sport because, if a player makes one mistake in baseball, it is crucial. When a mistake happens, it may cause his team to lose the game. Ladies, in baseball, every "Error" is recorded.

In baseball, after there are three outs, teams take turns and give each other the opportunity to score a run. This is why, after 3 outs you would see baseball players run off the field. Once three outs are obtained, the same players who play on defense must line up to bat and try to score a run for their team. Once they get three outs, they would then go back out and play defense, giving the other team the opportunity to score a run. When both teams have the opportunity to score a run, the innings change. So, once one team has the opportunity to score, and the other team has the opportunity to score, there would be an all new inning. This repeats itself until all 9 innings has been played. At the end of the game, the team that scores the most runs wins the game. To get a full understanding of baseball, like all sports, it's best to watch the game!!

Baseball Offence in plain English

Ladies, in baseball, the object is to score a run. To be able to score a run, a player must play offense. Once a player is on offense, he must first line up to hit the ball. He becomes a hitter, and the Pitcher throws the ball to him trying to strike him out. Once the hitter hit the ball, and he scores a run, one point is recorded for his team on the scoreboard. A baseball hitter may hit the ball out of the ball park, and when this happens, this is considered to be a homerun. A homerun is worth 1 point, unless there are other runners on base. For example, if a man is batting and a couple of his team mates or on 1st base and 2nd base and on 3rd base, after the homerun is hit, the team would record 4 points; one for the homerun and one for every player who was on base.

Batter—The man who hit the ball.

Base Runner—This is when the baseball player gets on base. He becomes a Base Runner.

Pinch Hitter—This is the man who is a substitute for the batter. Sometimes, a batter may not be a great batter, and the baseball coach may substitute the batter for someone better and this batter is called the pinch hitter.

Baseball Defense in plain English

Three outfielders—These are the men who catch the ball after it is hit out in the outfield. There is a man in the middle of the field; on the right side of the field and on the left side of the field.

1st base player—This man never leaves first base. Once the batter hits the baseball, a player will throw to first base and try to obtain an out for his team.

2nd base player—This player usually does not always stand on 2nd base unless there is a baseball runner on the base. If there is not a runner on this base, the 2nd base player will play off of the base in hopes that he can catch the ball after a hitter hits the ball to him. He will usually stand in between 2nd base and 1st base.

3rd base player—This player usually does not leave third base.

Shortstop—This person resides between second base and third base. After the batter hits the ball, the shortstop usually gets a lot of balls hit his way. After the short stop catches the ball, he will try his best to throw the ball to 1st base and get the hitter out.

Catcher—This is the man who stands behind the batter. This man has on the funny looking mask. He is there to catch the ball after the pitcher throws the ball trying to strike out the batter. The Catcher will also throw the ball to his 1st, 2nd or 3rd basemen trying to get a runner out.

Pitcher—This is the man who throws the ball to the batter. He tries to strike the batter out by throwing curve balls, fast balls, knuckle balls, etc. The pitcher's primary role is to throw a ball where the batter cannot hit it, causing the batter to strike out.

Things to know in Baseball

How many Strikes does a Batter get?—A Batter gets 3 strikes, and after these 3 strikes, the batter is out. Once a Pitcher strikes out a batter, the Pitcher receives a Strike Out or a "K" statistic. In baseball, the "K" represents a strike out.

What is a Ball?—Once a Batter receives 4 balls, he will automatically get to walk to 1ˢᵗ Base. Once the Pitcher throws 4 pitches that are not strikes, they are said to be Balls.

What is a Full Count in Baseball?—This is when the Pitcher has 2 Strikes and 3 Balls. If the Pitcher throws one more Ball for a total of 4 balls, the Batter will walk to 1ˢᵗ base, but if the Pitcher throws a ball to the Batter and the Batter fails to hit the ball, the Batter will receive his 3ʳᵈ strike. Once the Batter receives his 3ʳᵈ strike, the Pitcher has a Strike Out.

What is Hit by a Pitch?—This is self explanatory. This is when a Batter is hit by a Pitch, and he automatically gets on 1ˢᵗ base.

Does a Pitcher pitch every game?—A Pitcher does not pitch every game. A pitcher may pitch 1 game, and after he pitches that one game, he may rest every 3-5 days before he can pitch again.

What is a Closer?—In baseball, the Closer is a well rested Pitcher that comes in and throw Pitches in the 8ᵗʰ or the 9ᵗʰ innings. In baseball, the Closer is refreshed, and he usually throws great pitches and strike out Batters of the opposing teams.

What is a Double Play?—This is when there are two outs in one play. Once a player hits the ball, the defensive player may throw the ball to second base getting the second base runner out, and then the second base defensive player will then throw the ball to first base and get the first base runner out.

What is a Grand Slam?—This is when the Batter hits a Home Run when all of his teammates are on all of the bases. So, if players are on 1ˢᵗ, 2ⁿᵈ and 3ʳᵈ base, and a Batter comes to bat, and he hits a home run, that player who hit the home run has just hit a Grand Slam.

What is a Bunt?—A bunt is when the Batter connects his bat with the ball, but he doesn't fully swing at the ball.

What is a Foul Ball?—A Foul Ball is when the Batter hit the ball out of play. The ball lands on the outside of the lines of the bases, usually behind home plate, as well as on the outer side of 1ˢᵗ and 3ʳᵈ base.

Why do catchers have on a mask?—This is to protect him from getting hit by a ball thrown by the pitcher.

How long is a baseball game?—A baseball game is usually 9 innings; usually 3 hours. There is no time clock in baseball. There is a Top of the inning and Bottom of the inning. For example, in the 1ˢᵗ inning, team A will have a chance to score, and in the Bottom of the inning, Team B has a chance to score. After each team have a chance to score, then the ball game moves to another inning. 1st, 2nd, 3rd . . . . etc.

What is a "RBI?"—RBI simply means, "Runs Batted In." Ladies, if a batter is up to bat, and one of his team members is on base, and after he hits the ball, his team mate runs to all the way to home base and scores, the person who hit the ball receives an RBI. For example, if you were batting the ball and one of your teammates were on 3rd base, and after you hit the ball, your teammate has the opportunity to score without you receiving an out, you would receive an RBI.

What does the "K" symbol mean?—This is when the picture gets a strike out.

What does the "R" symbol mean?—This is the number of times the baseball team scores.

What does the "H" symbol mean?—This is the number of times the baseball team gets on 1st base.

What does the "E" symbol mean?—This is the number of times a team has made errors throughout the game.

What is a Batting Average?—When men watch baseball, we watch for batting averages. A really great batting average is .400, but in Major League Baseball, most good player's batting averages are around .300. The batting averages are the percentage that the batter connects with the ball. According to "Baseball-Reference.com," Babe Ruth's highest batting average was .378, and this occurred in 1924 when he was with the New York Yankees. Babe Ruth is known as one of the greatest Baseball hitters of all time. So, when a batter has a .300 batting average, that player has an above average batting average.

What is a No Hitter?—This is when no team hits the ball to get on base. For example, if a team can't hit a ball thrown by the pitcher, at the end of the game, the pitcher will have a "No Hitter."

Women, the **Sports Cheat Sheet** should help you understand the in and outs of the top 3 American Sports. Most women don't like sports because they simply don't understand the sport. If you learn the language of these sports, your man will be very impressed, and this may make him commit to you at a faster rate, especially if he is a stern sports fan. As a couple, you all can sit and watch a football game without you being confused. A man loves when his woman sit and enjoy a game with him, and this Sports Cheat Sheet will help you get one step closer to your man. Although these are the 3 most popular sports, your man may be into Hockey, Tennis, Boxing, Mix Martial Art fighting or Golf, but what every sport he likes, it doesn't hurt to have a little knowledge about that sport. You will gain a lot of commitment points if you decide to learn your man's favorite sport!!!!

ACKNOWLEDGEMENTS

First and foremost, I want to thank the creator for blessing me with the gift of poetry and giving me the ability to write it. With God, anything is possible. I also want to thank the many women who motivated and inspired me to write these poetic pieces; *you all know who you are.* To the women who read my poetry and gave me the necessary feedback that I needed, I want to thank you. To all of my homeboys, thanks for giving me the insight to write this book. I also want to thank *Shutterstock* for providing me with the images that was used throughout this book. Most of all, I want to thank my paternal grandparents who taught me the true meaning of love, and how a couple can stay committed until God calls you home.

Mr. Albert and Dave Vee Smith
May you two forever Rest in Peace, and one day I will see you all again.

I will always love you.